ELECTRIC GUITAR
DESIGN

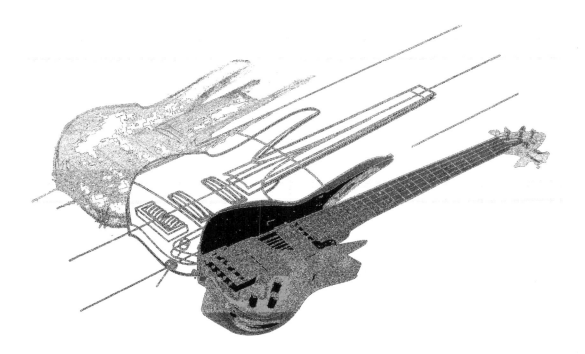

The guitar or bass of your dreams,
from the first draft to the full plan

Leonardo Lospennato

CREDITS

Many of the pictures used in this book come from flickr.com. Credit is given for each photo, which are here reproduced with the permission of the rights holders.

The properties of the different species of wood used in lutherie are reproduced with the permission of these websites: www.woodworkerssource.com, www.woodbin.com, www.woodzone.com

The chapter about pickups contains paragraphs reproduced with the permission of GM Arts (www.gmarts.com), to whom I express my gratitude.

Credits for pictures on Evolution of design table: © Pradi, © Tund, © Newlight, © Alxpin, © Vince Mo, © Funniefarm..., © Alexroz, all at www.dreamstime.com; www.flickr.com/photos: groovenite, purpleslog, glauser, lifeontheedge, x-ray_deta_one, imuttoo, hiddenloop, all CC BY-SA 2.0. From www.fotolia.com, © Michael Shake, © Marco Birn, © Imagery Majestic, © Evgeny Rannev, © jackrussell, © Denis Tabler, Detlev Dördelmann.

Sources for color meanings chart:

http://desktoppub.about.com/cs/color/a/symbolism.htm

http://www.squidoo.com/colorexpert

I thank **Axes-r-us Bodies** (www.axesrus.com) for allowing me to use photos taken from their site.

All guitar brands (Fender, Gibson, Rickenbacker, Ibanez, Yamaha, etc.) are property of the respective rights holders.

Likewise, all model names (Stratocaster, Les Paul, Telecaster, Explorer, Iceman, Tune-O-Matic, etc.) are property of the respective rights holders.

At the moment this book was finished I have no affiliation with any of the companies or brands here listed.

The ideas in this book are either original, or come from notes I scribbled well before I had any intention to publish them; that is the reason why some source citations might be missing. I simply no longer remember where I took those ideas from. If you are, or know, the author or rights holder of any content in this book, please write an email and I will gladly include the source in future editions; the same is valid for comments and interesting information.

CAUTION: It is the reader's responsibility to adopt all safety measures when working with tools (especially power tools) and other materials.

COPYRIGHT

ISBN 978-3-00-029642-0

First edition, February 2010

Visit my website! www.lospennato.com

ACKNOWLEDGMENTS

... First and foremost, to **R.M. Mottola**, *who generously shared his knowledge and experience. Without his wise advice, this book would not have had any chance to be what it finally got to be.*

....those who I call "my masters" (even if I never met them), who wrote the classic books on lutherie: **William Cumpiano, Dan Erlewine** *and* **Melvyn Hiscock; Tim Olsen,** *the* **American Lutherie Magazine,** *and the* **Guild of American Luthiers** (www.luth.org).

...the luthiers, specialized journalists, and distributors who shared their feedback with me: **Jens Ritter, Gerald Marleaux; Martin Roseman** *and* **Thomas Bowlus** *from Bass Gear Magazine (U.S.);* **Dirk Groll** *and* **Florian Erhart** *from* **Gitarre & Bass magazine** *(Germany).*

... **Helmuth Lemme,** *for his expert advice regarding pickups and electronics, and for allowing me to include here some content taken from his excellent book "Elektrogitarren—Technik und Sound".*

... the designers, luthiers, authors and musicians who shared with me their ideas on guitar design: **Ned Steinberger, Bob Shaw, Claudio** *and* **Claudia Pagelli, Martin Off, Ralf Martens** *and* **Sebastian Heck, Rick Toone, Jerome Little, Ola Strandberg,** *and* **Marc Dehnke.**

.... **Peter Borowski** *and* **ABM** (www.ABM-mueller.com), **Olaf Nobis,** *and* **Banzai Effects** (www.banzaieffects.com) *for allowing me to use their photos. ABM is among the finest producers of bridges, tailpieces, and other hardware for guitar and basses, and Banzai is the place you go if you have to buy guitar's electronic components in Germany.*

... **Frank Benthaus,** *who finishes my guitars like no one else.*

... My friend **Michael Göing,** *who designed the cover.*

... **Dieter Stork,** *author of the photo reproduced in the cover of this book, by his courtesy (originally published in the* **Gitarre & Bass magazine).**

... the readers that pointed out corrections and suggested improvements: **Axel Proschko, Johannes Hofer,** and **Martin Koch,** from www.buildyourownguitar.com.

... my family and friends for their love and support: My mother, **Marta Oneto;** *my father* **Héctor Lospennato, Silvana** *and* **Franco Lospennato; Juan Figari, Marta Polastri, Baltazar Avendaño Rímini, Héctor Schauvinhold, Gianfranco Conte, Matthew Ferguson, Dirk Welsch-Lehmann, Neil Corteen, Lina Shushulova, Angel Oneto** *and* **Silvia Lucarini** *(favorite uncle and aunt!) and family,* **Juanfe Rehm, Anika Wechsung** *and* **Sasha Wechsung.**

ABOUT THE AUTHOR

Text and photo: A. Figari

Leonardo Lospennato *was born in Buenos Aires in '68–at the heart of an Italian family. He lives in Berlin, Germany, with his wife* **Andrea** *and with* **Tango***, their black miniature schnauzer.*

Son of a manager and an artist, Leo became a bit of both when he started designing instruments and setting up a company to bring them to the market.

Curious by nature and inspired by a Renaissance spirit, he became a computer engineer, pursued a masters degree in marketing and management, worked many years for companies like IBM and eBay on both sides of the Atlantic, and published articles as a journalist–all while adding English, Italian and German languages to his native Spanish along the way. Truth be told, the "Renaissance spirit" also shows up in the form of a shameless affair he maintains with Italian cuisine–a mix of heritage and hobby.

But in the whole of this history, what remains a leitmotiv is his passion for the ancient art of creating musical instruments, an infatuation that began when he put together his first bass, at 16.

Creating something out of nothing. Searching for meaning. Chasing the utopia of perfection.

Being a designer does not require much more than that. Nor anything less.

*To my wife **Andrea**,*
love of my life.

CONTENTS AT A GLANCE

(Detailed table of contents: see page 215)

WELCOME

This book is about the electric guitar or bass you are planning to build. It deals with the decisions to make *before* you cut any wood. **It is a book about inspiration, creativity, and the search for beauty.**

This is a book for luthiers and musicians, both amateur and professional, on designing guitars that look great, play great, and sound fantastic.

The usual advice is to start with a simple model, leaving the most ambitious designs for a later time: *"You might fail!"* But this book advises starting with whatever you want. Go ahead; design the guitar of your dreams! Draw a bass in the shape of a genetic cross between a bat and a banana, if you want. There are way too many Stratocaster copies around, anyway.

Your future guitars will come up better, though. And if you keep building these things, you will have been hypnotized by this arcane art called *lutherie*. Of all the hobbies available, you have chosen a very challenging one. *Couldn't you think of something else?* Astronomy, philately, yoga. Those are fun, aren't they?

But **lutherie**... oh, lutherie has it all. Lutherie is inspiring, is frustrating, is rewarding, is deeply technical, is highly artistic... it is like nothing else. And you get to hold in your hands something made by you, an object you can make music with.

And what happens if the thing doesn't play in tune, or if it's as ugly as a genetic cross between a bat and a banana? Nothing, really. Just hide it somewhere and start another one. Learning is all about trials and errors. *Your* errors–the only ones you can learn from.

So, welcome, and thanks for reading. Imagine that **Antonio de Torres**, **Hermann Hauser**, and **Leo Fender** are right there, sitting with you, commenting and giving you support as you go. Let's be humbly inspired by their example, then we will have already succeeded.

Enjoy!

Berlin, Germany, February 2010

INTRODUCTION

"When your mother asks, 'Do you want a piece of advice?' it is a mere formality. It doesn't matter if you answer yes or no. You're going to get it anyway."

– Erma Bombeck (American humorist, 1927-1996)

Who is this book for?

This book has been written for:

- **The musician,** an electric guitar or bass player who is looking for a different kind of instrument, one that cannot be found in music shops. He looks for originality and personalization. He knows that he cannot stand apart from the crowd if the instrument hanging around his neck is exactly the same as that of many other million people.
- **The hobbyist,** who has already built a few guitars, but is looking for a more professional way to go through the process, a way that respects the knowledge he has already accumulated.
- **The professional luthier,** someone with extensive experience in guitar design and guitar making, but who stays open to new ideas.

What should you get from this book?

Peter Drucker, the renowned marketing guru, said: *"Every moment spent in planning saves three or four in execution"*. An electric guitar is a very complex object, with 200 or so individual parts. Its quality is highly dependent on multiple, very precise relations among these elements. Planning is critical to achieving a quality result.

For that reason, this book will accompany you during the most important phase of the project: the development of a raw idea into a complete, professional specification–**the design.**

By the time you finish the book, you should have:

- A clear idea of the instrument you want to build.
- Enough knowledge to create a fully detailed blueprint of your new design.
- A list of the materials and parts you must buy or build.
- An enjoyable, creative experience!

What this book is *not* about

This is not a recipe book. This is a "how to" book, but only up to a point. I will do my best to show you the options; you will make the decisions. This book has a precise structure, though, to guide your focus.

Most guitar making books start discussing wood. This book *ends* discussing wood. This book is about what you need to know *before* you start building the guitar of your dreams. This book is...

- **Not** about guitar *making*–as in "woodworking". It is about guitar *design*: building a **great guitar** requires a **great plan.**

- **Not** about electronics–as in how to solder or hand-wind pickups. It is about designing a great interface player/instrument, and translating *that* into the necessary electronics.

- **Not** about guitar finishing–as in mixing solvents and sanding coats. It is about deciding which finish will better convey the aesthetic, acoustic, and symbolic attributes of our new instrument.

How is this book organized?

Parts

- **Part I–Searching for the Perfect Guitar** is about **inspiration**, and the objectives of excellent guitar design: **beauty, playability, and sound**.

- **Part II** - is about **aesthetics.** It focuses on the design of the **body** and the **headstock**; it is about originality and the quest for beauty.

- **Part III** is about **playability.** It deals with ergonomics, balance, and the subtleties of the **neck** and the **fretboard**.

- **Part IV** is about finding an excellent **sound.** How to select, match, and place **pickups**. It also focuses on **control** design: How many, which ones, located where, and why.

- **Part V** is about **materials** and **guitar and bass parts**. It tells you how to select the **wood** and the right **hardware** for your new instrument.

- **Part VI** contains only one chapter: **how to draw the blueprint of your new guitar.**

Chapters

In most chapters you will find the following structure:

- **"The basics":** presents the stuff that experienced readers presumably already know, but that is indispensable for beginners.

- **"In depth":** this is where we immerse ourselves in the real discussion. Here you will find most of the original content of this book.

- **"The checklist":** summarizes the chapter and includes some final, additional ideas and recommendations–these are the notes I took so you don't have to.

Appendixes

At the end of the book you will find interviews with several renowned guitar designers from the U.S. and Europe, sharing their thoughts on **beauty, playability, sound, inspiration and originality**, plus information on wood species used in lutherie, pickups dimensions, and pickup wiring color codes.

Things you will need

The last chapter of this book will give you the advice you need to draw a complete, real-size blueprint of your new design: that is the tangible outcome of this book. But the previous chapters, in the meantime, will stimulate your creativity: that is where the real design process takes place. You have to keep a record of all the things that will come to your mind as you go (ideas, concepts, reminders, etc.) in the form of sketches and notes. So you will need:

- **A mechanical pencil**. Use soft leads, 2B as a minimum. Do not use hard pencils: the lines are hard to see and hard to erase, and pressure will leave marks on the paper. I recommend not using common pencils, either.

- **A ruler.** For the moment, use a short, transparent one. You will need a longer ruler to draw the blueprint, though.

- **Paper.** For the blueprint, which needs a lot of precision, you can use *quadrille* (graph paper). For the moment, you just need blank, letter size paper. Don't buy cheap paper: it has a shiny surface to which the pencil particles don't hold well, so you will stain the paper and yourself. Normal paper sheets for printers or copiers will suffice.

- **An eraser.** Or three.

Icons used in this book

Practical advice

Represents a "quick exit": the cheapest, fastest, simplest way to do things.

Cool Idea!

It highlights innovations, examples of "thinking out of the box", and clever ideas.

Worst case scenario

Whenever you see this icon, pay special attention. It warns you about things that could ruin the design, or be harmful to yourself or others.

Standard measurements

Under this icon you will find the standard measurements used in classic guitar and bass models; they will serve as references for your own design.

Web resources

It points you to useful resources on the Internet.

For perfectionists

The paragraphs identified with this icon contain comments at very subtle detail levels. Their contribution is marginal; just skip them if you want.

Personal opinion!

A book speaks with the voice of its author, so being subjective is unavoidable. But this icon will identify paragraphs which content is particularly influenced by the author's personal preferences.

Worth saying

Just as I include both genders in the masculine pronouns (repeating *"he or she"* all the time is disturbing for both writer and reader) each time I refer to "guitars" I am including basses, too—except when specifically noted or when obvious by the context of the discussion. Also, when I say "you", I refer to "you, or your customer".

Last but not least

This is not a perfect book: It is –humbly– the best book I could write. I am sure there are things missing, things I got wrong, things that are incomplete. And when the author can't find anything more to be improved, the reader surely will.

So, if you believe I should add, correct, change or eliminate something, please send me an email to: leo@lospennato.com**.** I enjoy reading and answering them all.

If your contribution is accepted, I will gratefully add your name on each copy of the book from then on. I thank you in advance! [1]

---

[1] *English is not my first language, so please tell me about typos, too!*

Part I

Searching for the perfect guitar

1: Inspiration

It all starts with the spark of inspiration. We review two guitar models (the Gibson Les Paul and the Fender Stratocaster), which represent two different, classic paradigms of guitar design. They will be our references when discussing practically every topic in the book (also relevant to basses, of course).

2: Uniting form and function

An object of design must fulfill a mission (its usability), which sometimes competes with the harmony and beauty of the forms. This chapter is about fusing form and function together, to achieve a functional and attractive concept. This chapter also establishes the terminology to be used throughout the book, naming not only the parts of the guitar, but also the shapes, lines, volumes and recesses.

3: Beauty, playability, and sound

This chapter reviews the components of a guitar from the standpoint of their contribution to the "trinity" of guitar design: appealing beauty, excellent playability and a killer sound.

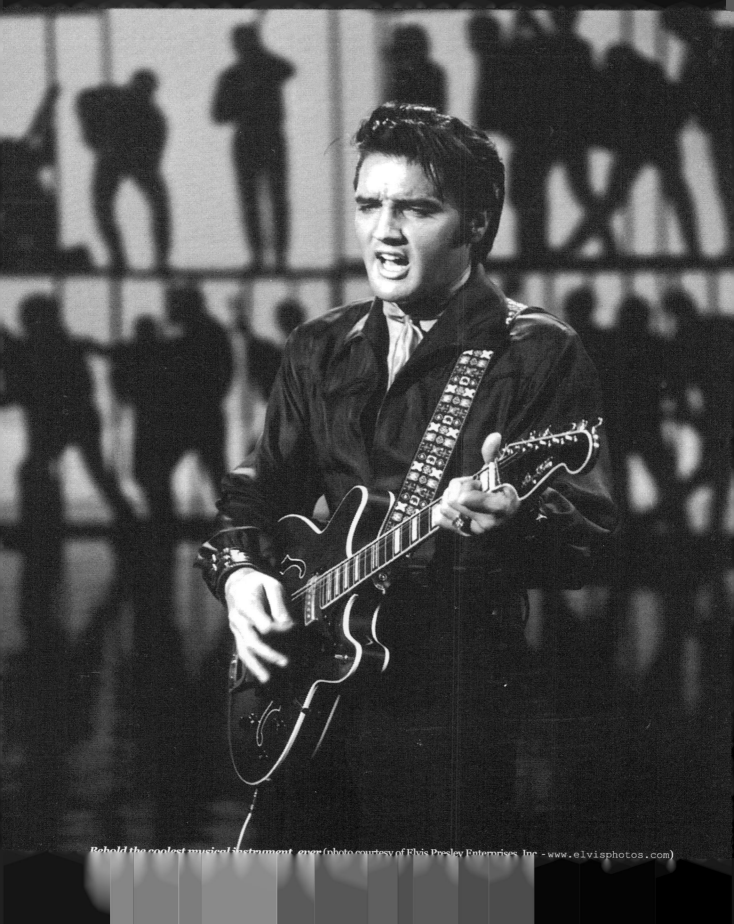

Behold the coolest musical instrument, ever (photo courtesy of Elvis Presley Enterprises, Inc - www.elvisphotos.com)

INSPIRATION

- **Sources of inspiration: keeping mind and eyes wide open**
- **Timeless beauty: Les Pauls and Stratocasters**
- **The dark side of the classics**

Look at your car. Just look at it. Now look at your neighbor's. Can you tell them apart? In the 50's, the 60's, into the 70's, your car was an individual statement. Your car had style, character, panache. It had curves and edges, came in a myriad of colors and could be personalized in a million ways. [Now] everybody drives the same car, the Generica. You go on long highway drives now, and every Generica around you looks just like the Generica you're in.

—John Strausbaugh, "Sissy Nation" (Virgin Books, 2007).

Where does inspiration come from?

Some electric guitars have been so popular, for so long, with so many copies and imitations, that by now they are like the *Generica* of guitars.

We will dissect and analyze the classics: the famous guitar models will serve us for comparison and example throughout the book. But using them as references for your own designs is too strong a conditioning influence. In order to create something original, you have to get inspiration from anything and from everything. The design of a new classic demands detachment from the old ones.

I frequently draw inspiration from automobiles, like those magnificent Chrysler and De Soto concept cars that never made it into mass production. Or from architecture, or even from cartoons. Good art books can be inspiring, as they depict the most beautiful examples from different historical periods. Not that you are going to design a bass with the face of the Mona Lisa on it (are you?). It's the *spirit* of those masterpieces that could start the flame of creativity.

Sometimes inspiration comes not from a particular object, but from the example of other creative people, from the most varied disciplines. I get inspiration from the music of **Imogen Heap**, a superb British singer. Or old **J.S. Bach**. Now, what's the relationship between a Bach cantata and a guitar? None evident. The secret resides in the underlying class and genius of those creations. A painting could be inspiring. A watch. An old radio set. A poem.

Did you know? Creatively expressing ourselves can bring meaning to our lives. Or at least that's what **Viktor Frankl** said. Dr. Frankl was the author of a small book titled *Man's Search for Meaning*—not just another book, but one of the top-ten, all-time most influential books in America, according to the U.S. Library of Congress. Apparently, building an electric bass is not only fun, but it could cure your neuroses, too.

Paul Reed Smith, luthier and founder of PRS Guitars, said *"Leo Fender was in a state of grace when he created the Stratocaster"*. What inspired Leo? Was it another guitar? Maybe it was a girl—a guitar has the shape of a woman, in case you haven't noticed.

Anything is potentially inspiring—we just have to keep our eyes open.

The charm of the six strings

All musical instruments carry their own *aura*. They used to call the church organ the *Rex Instrumentorum* ("the king of instruments"), a well-deserved nickname for such a magnificent musical device. The piano is probably the most versatile and expressive modern instrument, and the possibilities offered by its descendants the electronic keyboards are virtually unlimited. And then we have the violins, of course: they are the most mythical of all instruments, which allegedly still contain undiscovered construction secrets.

But the Electric Guitar.... Oh, the electric guitar is simply the coolest of all instruments. Ever. And the electric bass is her big brother.

Do you think otherwise? Well, you must play some mean bagpipe, or whatever it is that you play. And you sure look cooler with it than Elvis playing a Hagstrom Viking II (see page 14).

What's a bagpipe, anyway? A sheep's stomach or something, in which you blow air... *Nah, there's nothing like an electric guitar.*

The simple magic of a timeless beauty

And among all guitars, two models are the most popular: The **Gibson Les Paul** and the **Fender Stratocaster**.

The Gibson Les Paul

The Les Paul is a simple, elegant design, with rounded *bouts* which are reminiscent of classical guitars (we will see what a "bout" is, very soon). It was designed by **Lester Polsfuss** (1915-2009)—who later took his stage name, *Les Paul*—an American jazz guitarist and inventor, one of the most important figures in the development of both modern musical instruments and recording techniques.

Les Paul at 93, playing live the all-time bestseller signature guitar model: his. (Photo: Amy Tragethon).

The final shape of the Les Paul model though, is believed to have been developed at Gibson. Les Paul's first solid body electric guitar design was made in the 40's and consisted of a piece of solid wood, a 4x4" pine block, with two halves of a semi hollow guitar attached to it, to give the visual impression of a normal guitar. The instrument was known as "The Log", and it probably was as heavy as one.

A solid body instrument resolved two main problems of amplifying a guitar:

- **Feedback**, as there was no acoustic body resonating with the amplifier.
- **Sustain**, as the energy of the strings was not dissipated through the bridge into the top, like in an acoustic guitar.

The Fender Stratocaster

Leo Fender, holding that magic pencil (Photo by Bob Perine, copyrighted and used by permission of Blaze Newman).

The other timeless classic is the Fender Stratocaster. It has the most popular guitar body shape, and is still the weapon of choice for a never-ending list of players. It was designed in the early 50's by **Clarence Leonidas ("Leo") Fender, George Fullerton,** and **Freddy Tavares**, with the collaboration of several musicians. It is said that the name "Stratocaster" was intended to evoke images of the powerful new bomber, the B-52 "Stratofortress". To me, "Strat" also evokes "stratosphere"–the space race had just begun–and "Strad", short for "Stradivarius". The *"-caster"* part was already used by Fender in previous models (as in the "Broadcaster" model, later claimed by Gretsch as a registered trademark of a drumset of theirs, and so renamed to "Telecaster"). The innovative body shape was designed with a tummy bevel, and an arm bevel. They represented the most innovative take on electric guitar ergonomics up to that moment. The double cutaway, the tremolo, and other great ideas made this guitar into a catalog of good product design.

The dark side of the classics

The astonishing fact about both these models is that they went through all these decades virtually unchanged. A 1954 Les Paul and a 2004 Les Paul present no differences in shape or size. Some hardware changed; colors and details and maybe even quality changed. But not the design: it's virtually the same guitar. If we look at a Stratocaster, we cannot tell for sure if it is a real '67 or if it is a reissue made yesterday—at least not from the design itself. Very few products can withstand the test of time in such a way.

There is a dark side, though. The classic models are the queens among the guitars, but also the example that all *Genericas* out there follow by imitation, or just plain copy.

"Since guitars were electrified, they became a symbol for freedom and rebellion against outdated rules. But they aren't free or rebellious anymore. For fifty years guitars have been wearing the same clothes and have been following the same rules. The former rebel is now itself part of the establishment", reads the website www.gitarrendesign.de. I think they have a point.

A consumerist society generates objects which, while beautiful, become *kitsch* by over-consumption. "Kitsch" is a term that denotes an inferior, tasteless copy of elements (usually with the rank of cultural icons), producing –or *mass* producing– unoriginal results. Such objects can be beautiful—until they become so fashionable that the initial sense of exclusivity degenerates into ubiquity. Strats and Les Paul's are not kitsch (most of them aren't, anyway). But they (and specially their copies) are certainly over-consumed.

Are Strats and Les Pauls the best guitars? "Bestseller" doesn't necessarily mean *best*. Many decades have passed since their introduction, and a lot of improvements have been made since then. As with most subjects dealt with in this book, deciding which guitar is the best will always be a matter of personal taste. Who knows? Maybe you will design a new classic, to be used from now on and through the 22nd century.

Okay, maybe not. But trying is still a lot of fun.

Checklist

Finding inspiration

- Any artistic or technical discipline (not necessarily related to guitars) can be inspiring. Look for inspiration in those pieces of creation you admire or enjoy.
- Try to transcend the superficial attributes (color, motifs, brands, fashion, popularity) and look for the underlying essence: proportion, meaning, details, functionality, style.

● Historically successful models are not necessarily perfect. Take advantage of the lessons they offer, but be open to find new paths. Les Pauls and Stratocasters are considered "traditional" today, but when they were created, they were radical examples of innovation themselves.

Evolution of design: Hats & Strats

	Telephones	Computers	Concept Cars	Her Majesty's hats	Strats
50's					
60's					
70's					
80's					
90's					
00's					

(Photo credits on page 33)

The evolution of some popular products through the decades. Good design persists unaltered through the decades; the question is: Does that justify resigning innovation?

An awarded guitar model designed by Martin Off, the "Glamour Babe" (Photo reproduced by his courtesy).

UNITING FORM AND FUNCTION

- **The traditional anatomy: Parts and components**
- **The "design" anatomy: Lines, curves, shapes**
- **Anatomy of the back side of a guitar**
- **Usability vs. looks in guitar design**
- **The powerful role of decoration**

"– The next sign is "C2". What do you make of that, Watson?

– 'Chapter the second', no doubt.

– Hardly that, Watson. You will, I am sure, agree with me that [...] if page 534 finds us only in the second chapter, the length of the first one must have been really intolerable."

– From "Sherlock Homes–The Valley of Fear", by A. Conan Doyle

The basics

Electric guitar anatomy

Sure enough, you are already familiar with the electric guitar's anatomy that is presented in the following page. It is the *traditional* anatomy of a guitar, an enumeration of parts and pieces. But check out the *design* anatomy that comes after. It offers a design-oriented view of an electric guitar or bass, focused on form and function. (You may want to mark the next couple of pages, to use them for future reference).

Anatomy of a guitar (traditional version)

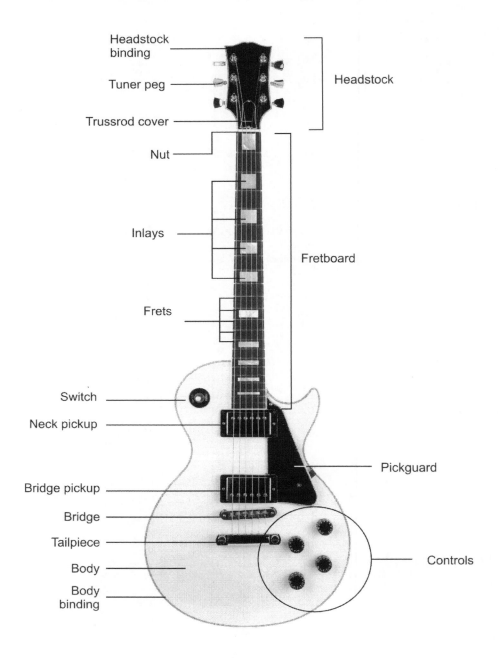

Headstock binding

Tuner peg

Trussrod cover

Nut

Headstock

Inlays

Fretboard

Frets

Switch

Neck pickup

Pickguard

Bridge pickup

Bridge

Tailpiece

Body

Body binding

Controls

Anatomy of a guitar (design version)

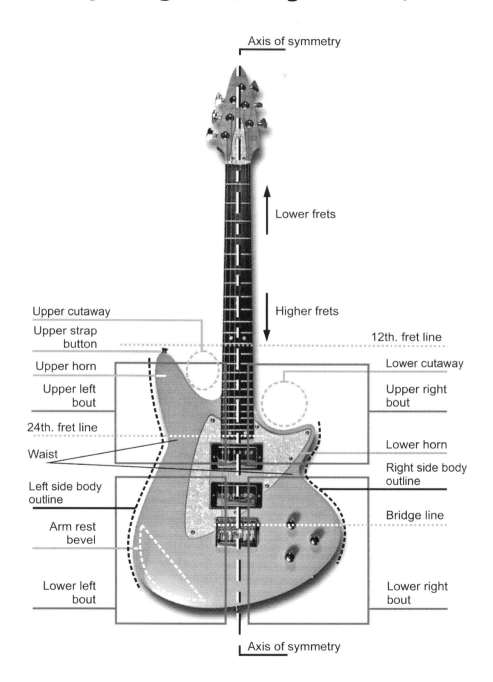

Axis of symmetry

Lower frets

Upper cutaway

Upper strap button

Higher frets

12th. fret line

Upper horn

Lower cutaway

Upper left bout

Upper right bout

24th. fret line

Waist

Lower horn

Left side body outline

Right side body outline

Arm rest bevel

Bridge line

Lower left bout

Lower right bout

Axis of symmetry

Photo: www.lospennato.com

Anatomy of the back (design version)

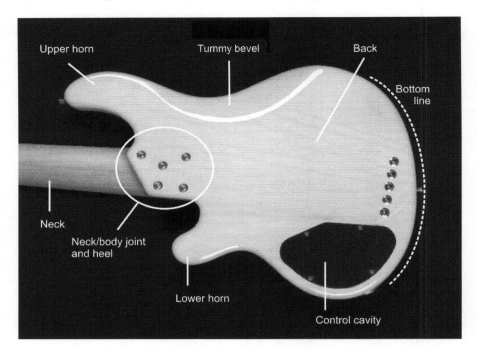

Upper horn · Tummy bevel · Back · Bottom line · Neck · Neck/body joint and heel · Lower horn · Control cavity

Visibility vs. usability

Should electric guitars be beautiful, or should they be playable? What's more important in a bass: the looks, or the touch? The engineers' favorite answer applies: *"it depends"*. It depends on the kind of guitar you are planning to build; on the objectives you defined for your design.

Prioritizing form (beauty, aesthetics, representation, symbolism, and message) is appropriate to an artistic evaluation. If I see a sculpture, a painting or other object of art, sooner or later my judgment of it will relate to its beauty. But if I am evaluating a can opener, for example, I don't care if it is the ugliest thing in the world: if it works fine, then it is fine. Being a tool, the first evaluation criterion is not aesthetical. Function (usability, practicality, ergonomics, performance, safety, portability) takes precedence.

"Form follows function" is a design principle which gained popularity in the last few decades: it is associated with modern architecture and industrial design (the shape of a building or object should be primarily based upon its intended function or purpose). Intuitively, this seems like good sense, but its application might not extend to other areas of design. A guitar, for example, is more than just a tool; it is more than just its musical function alone. It is also something that:

- Must fit our body (it is something we *use*, but it is also something we almost *wear*)
- Becomes part of the player's image
- Reflects our personality as designers
- In some instances of excellence, it can reach the level of *art*

So, in a guitar, form and function can't precede each other: they must *serve* each other.

Decoration

Decoration, or ornamentation, has been the subject of engaged debate in design. **Adolf Loos**, an Austrian modernist architect, wrote in *Ornament and Crime*, in 1908:

> *"I reject the argument that ornamentation increases the pleasures of life of a cultivated person, or that it is beautiful. [...] Ornamented objects appear unaesthetic [even] if executed in the best material with much labor time. [...] Someone who listens to Beethoven and then works on wallpaper patterns is degenerate".*

Incendiary rhetoric, also common in other modernist manifestos from the early 1900's—a reaction to the previous centuries' saturated styles (baroque, rococo, etc.). Modernism intended to be a deconstruction of those periods, reflected in styles like *Bauhaus*, deprived of ornamentation. A balance ensued, though, from about 1920 on, with the emergence of styles that today are also perceived as classic—i.e. Art Deco, Art Nouveau, etc.

The role of decoration

Has decoration any role in guitar design? Of course it does:

- It conveys personality to a design.
- It contributes to its aesthetic impact.
- It embodies a metaphor—it carries a message.
- It evokes associations.

Such an association can sometimes be *nausea*, of course. But just as decoration can play a role in architecture (to help wayfinding, announcing the identity of a building, attracting customers inside, for example), it can also play a functional role in other applications, too.

Decoration in a guitar can undoubtedly reinforce identity, both the player's and the maker's. Examples: **Randy Roads'** Polka-dots Flying V, **Zakk Wylde's** "Buzzsaw" Les Paul, or any of the highly decorated **Steve Vai** axes—just to name the guitars used by a few of Ozzy's band members.

Even something as basic as *color* is already decoration. Have you seen the "Hello Kitty" Stratocaster? It is an adorable, "girlie" guitar made by Squier. But paint it all black, and it becomes a hard-

(Photo: Andrew Stawarz)

It would take a real man to use one of these on stage!

rocker's instrument. Or just put a *SpongeBob SquarePants* sticker on it, and it becomes a child's guitar. Cover that sticker with a satanic one, and it will attract the attention of your average *death metal* musician.

I believe that beauty must emerge primarily from *form* and its relation to *function*, without over-relying on ornamentation, which is dictated by and vulnerable to fashion changes.

Traditional electric guitar decoration

The traditional resources used to ornament a guitar are:

- The **finish**.
- The **binding**,
- The use of **inlays** as fret markers.
- **Decals** (usually attached to the headstock)

Binding—the verb—is the action of applying a long stripe made of plastic or wood (called "binding"—noun) that runs along the perimeter of the guitar's body and fretboard. In acoustic instruments, it protects the top from moisture, preventing it from deforming too much with changes in humidity. In solid body guitars its role is merely ornamental.

In order to be able to apply binding, the guitar must have sharp edges, like the top edges of a Les Paul, not rounded-over edges like in a Stratocaster.

Inlay is the decorative technique of inserting pieces of plastic, mother of pearl or other shell into previously carved depressions. The inserted pieces, which normally are flush with the wood, form figures or simply decorative patterns or visual elements (for example, a logo or some other motif, symbol or drawing). Applying inlay is an art in itself. There are many good sources on this matter [2]. At the design stage, it is important to keep in mind the aesthetic aspect of it. Inlays are good examples of form, function and decoration fused together. The function of inlayed fretboard markers is to help the player's orientation on the fretboard, and their form *is* the decoration.

Advice about inlays: If you go for something complex, then it is interesting to make the *theme* of the inlays somehow related to the aesthetic conception or theme of the instrument. Good examples are the famous **B.B. King's** "Lucille", with B.B.'s signature inlayed on the fretboard, or the Gibson SG **Tony Iommi** Signature model, with inlays in the form of crosses, just like the pendant Tony wears.

Applying binding and inlays demand a lot of expertise and time. *If you have never done it before, do not start on a real instrument, but on scrap wood.* **Use a respirator and eye protection.** *The dust created by sawing mother of pearl, abalone and other shell may provoke silicosis, a disease so nasty I don't even want to tell you about it.*

Buy inlays already cut. Inlay the fretboard before it is glued to the neck, and before installing the frets. Practice before you work on the real thing!

Decals serve not only a decorative element, but also provide information about an instrument, for ex-

[2] *Pearl Inlay Book, By James E. Patterson; The Art of Inlay, by Larry Robinson, etc.*

ample to identify the brand, model, place of manufacturing and serial number. The most famous example is the "Fender" decal. Decals are a cheaper alternative to inlays, in terms of both cost and time.

In depth

The quest for beauty

Aesthetic perception is subjective. However, people who share a culture also share common ideas regarding what is beautiful and what is not, whether an object is classy or cheesy, whether something has creative value or not.

This is a very subtle matter, even an unconscious one. But beauty can be understood through attributes that are quantifiable in nature. Let's review some of these attributes.

Simplicity / complexity

I found the following definition of simplicity: *"the property or quality of an entity of being uncombined, free from hardship, effort or confusion"*. It is the opposite of complicated: "overloaded, with many elements or parts".

Current trends in design identify simplicity as a desirable attribute, and consider complexity to be outmoded. Simplicity and complexity are not good or bad in themselves, of course, but are a consequence of the function of the object we are designing. Simplicity can be a fashion, exactly as complexity was in fashion back in the baroque period. To be fair, let's say that a good design is as simple as it can be, without compromising other attributes as function, performance, controllability, safety, etc.

Identifying simplicity and complexity in everyday design is an interesting exercise. A classy watch will be essentially simple and sober. A classy, sporty watch will have more buttons and needles, but this complexity will be at the service of function and style. On the contrary, a watch with a huge logo, fluorescent colors, 4 different materials and melodies will appear as excessive, no matter how expensive it is. However, it can be perceived favorably by a particular audience, for example teenagers and rap singers. Taste will be always a subjective matter.

Note the difference between *complex* and *complicated*. So, complexity can be a good thing, even a necessary one. A jet engine is complex, and it can be superb in its complexity. But if it were more complex that it needs to be, it could lose efficiency, become too expensive, or unstable, due to a *superfluous* addition of complexity. What is a "complicated" guitar body shape? It is one with many inflexion points, forced curves, disproportioned protuberances, and unnatural-looking lines. A guitar doesn't have to be complicated or extreme to be radical and original. Take, for example, the Flying V. It has a very simple shape, but it is also full of character and personality. Complication arises when we try too hard to be original and end up with an instrument that is more radical than perhaps intended. The challenge is to achieve originality, while maintaining things just as simple as they can be. Except when we are trying to design something *deliberately* complex, of course.

John Maeda is the author of the book The Laws of Simplicity. The 10th law–which he calls "The One"–tells us: "Simplicity is about subtracting the obvious, and adding the meaningful". *A concept in sintony with* **Leonardo Da Vinci's** *thought:* "Simplicity is the ultimate sophistication".

A good design doesn't have to be *extreme* to stand out. It has to be *effective*. It definitely has to cause an impression, but a good one. It has to be as simple or complex as the function demands. The introduction of complication in the design, however, may resonate negatively in other aspects of the instrument.

Proportion

Relative size matters

Proportion refers to the size of the parts in relation to the whole, and the way they contribute to a pleasant perception of that whole. It is probably the most quantifiable component of beauty, and the key concept here is that of *ratio*.

Good proportion goes unnoticed as such, but is perceived as a certain harmony in the design. Bad proportion, instead, is noticed as some element, area or distance being too big or too small. Sometimes oddly proportioned designs are referred to as "cartoony" because cartoon characters are generally drawn out of proportion on purpose. This can be a good thing or a bad thing, depending of course on what your goal is for the design.

These are some guidelines for achieving good proportion:

- The first relation to consider is that between instrument and player. Who will play that bass? A regular sized person, a kid, or a 300+ lbs guy? [3]

- Elements which are similar in character should be placed in a clear relation to each other; for example, designing a multi-neck instrument with all neck ends, or all bridges, laying on a common line, etc. (see photo next page).

- Obvious mathematical relationships between elements, like halves, quarters and thirds are harmonic. But subtle proportions (the *golden ratio, for example,* discussed in chapter 4) are also useful.

Symmetry / Asymmetry

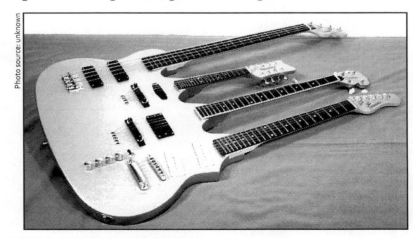

Photo source: unknown

A huge... "guitar", sold on eBay for 225 dollars, with 4 necks (guitar, bass, banjo and mandolin). Talk about proportions!

[3] *I am one of them, and of course I prefer bigger instruments!*

Is the *self-similarity* of an entity, perceptible through such geometric transformations as scaling, reflection, repetition and rotation. Symmetry is a natural character of beautiful things. The sun, a flower, ourselves. Symmetry is everywhere. But superior beauty can also be achieved through *asymmetry*. For example, the art of *Ikebana* (Japanese flower arrangement) is based on the line of twigs, leaves and blooms arranged on a scalene triangle. Some arrangements are composed of just three flowers, and no two of them lie on the same orthogonal plane. Ikebana arrangements

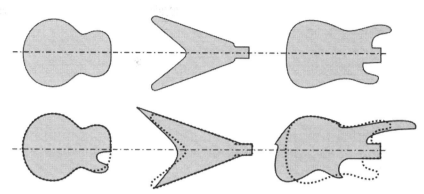

Compare the symmetrical body shapes at the top of the figure against their assymetric counterparts in the bottom row; note the dynamics that assymetry introduces.

are amazingly beautiful. So are Telecasters and Explorers and Jaguars, all of them asymmetric.

Let's stand in front of a mirror: we are symmetric beings, but only to a point. Perfect symmetry can be boring, or look too artificial. In nature, perfect symmetry is only found in minerals or ice crystals (and only there if you don't look too deep)–thus it can convey an idea of hardness, coldness, rigidity. In living organisms symmetry is imperfect, and our perception of beauty incorporates that imperfection as a natural component. Electric guitars are often asymmetric for good functional reasons: they need cutaways in order to allow access to the higher frets, and also because of balance-related issues. However, there are some really nice symmetric body shapes: the Flying V, the ES-335 and others of similar lines, some jazz guitars, many acoustic guitars, and all classical guitars. *What will your guitar be like?*

Visual balance

Visual balance is about *intrinsic equilibrium*, the harmonious distribution of the parts in relation to the whole in terms of placement and visual weight.

All these resources add to a visually balanced design:

- **Alignment**: position the elements in relation to a reference (a point, an axis, a line, a plane, or other components).

- **Repetition,** which is the essence of *patterns*. The repeated elements don't necessarily have to be identical: a beautiful example of repetition is the bird-inlays of the PRS guitars–all different, but all birds.

- **Proximity**: grouping elements– or isolating them– is a technique to emphasize, to create (or break) a visual bond among them.

Contrast

Contrast is created by using opposite values of a certain attribute, like color, size, shape, value, type, texture, alignment, or direction. The appropriate use of contrast breaks monotony, enriching the design. Too much contrast will produce undesired effects, though:

- **Excessive polarity**. Imagine painting a guitar with a sunburst pattern (dark on the outside, fading to a lighter color on the center of the body). The effect is much more intense (and confusing to the eye) if the change is too radical, for example fading from black to white, than if it goes from dark red to light red.

- **Fragmentation**. Imagine a guitar body that combines straight lines with curved ones. The contrast in the shapes would create the impression that a part of the body has been cut off in the parts where the straight lines are. A way to control the contrast would be to use subtle, wider curves instead of straight lines (more on body shape and curves on chapter 4).

- **Disproportion** is the way contrast would manifest if used in regard to size. For example, a very big guitar body with a very small (or no) headstock. That is probably why many headless instruments have also relatively small bodies.

Originality

Do you still want to build a copy of a Precision bass? I am sure it's going to be nice. But it isn't going to be original.

Originality is the unique attribute of something (an object, an idea, a concept) that didn't exist at all before. But we can also provide originality to our designs by applying old resources in new ways: reinterpretation, rediscovery, recombination, and reinvention. Your creativity in designing your guitar will be perceptible in the form of originality; it establishes a differentiation, it stands out. It provides identity to a design—and reinforces its creator's.

Classy or kitsch?

We said above that the perception of an artistic object (or any objects, in general) stimulates a judgement within us. To *know* something means to evaluate it, and guitars are no exception. *What is tasteful, and what is not?* French philosopher **Pierre Bourdieu** said: "the legitimate taste of a society is the taste of the ruling class". If the ruling class of music is formed by the famous stars, the instruments they play will be considered tasteful in that culture. More in general, though, we can value as "tasteful" those designs that allude to superior notions, ideas, or concepts. Beauty, sobriety, simplicity, unity, harmony, transcendence. On the contrary, something with "bad taste" remits to negative, inferior, culturally repressed notions.

A **classy** guitar will probably look exclusive, expensive, sober, masterfully built, perfectly finished, and with a delicate balance between originality and classicism. It will be different, even modern, but not radical to the point of conflicting with our established preferences. And, without necessarily falling in minimalism, it will be relatively *simple*.

I suspect that beauty reaches its highest potential when it emerges from abstraction, and that a guitar has to have the shape of a guitar, not the shape of something else. The kitsch, however, can be a deliberate objective of the design, to produce results that go beyond the function of the guitar as a mere musical instrument. Examples: a guitar in the shape of a mobile home, a tennis racquet, or the Space Shuttle, intending to achieve a humorous effect (which dissipates soon, though).

Taste is of course subjective. However, we can enumerate some suggestions to avoid bad taste (or to achieve it, if that is what you are looking for!):

- **Using spoiled, waste or bizarre materials,** for example, feathers, leather, and others of animal origin).[5] There is a contemporaneous trend to use recycled materials ("one man's rubbish is another man's treasure").

- **Ostentatious materials.** Materials that are too good or too costly; objects that "flaunt their wealth". Or the contemporary trend of covering the most mundane things with bling.

- **Fake materials,** like those leaves that imitate gold, or cubic zirconia passing for diamonds.

- **Material decoys.** Playful attempts to imitate things that are not really there. Example: bullet holes painted with an air brush. It is not easy to make something classy on a guitar with an air brush. This is a technique more adapted to other applications.

- **Relief transpositions,** such as three-dimensional representations of popular paintings (like the Mona Lisa carved on a guitar's top).

- **Patent humor** or other elements that attract attention at the expense of the main function.

- **Too much originality**, to the point that the result is contrived or excessive.

The guitar's design as a message

A guitar in the shape of a beautiful rifle can be ugly, or ineffective, as a guitar. But again, other scopes of the design can be at play. For example, Colombian luthier **Alberto Paredes** has built a series of electric guitars named *Escopetarras*[6] from decommissioned assault rifles. They are perfect examples of good design, but not necessarily from a lutherie point of view: they meet their intended political purpose so well that one of them is on permanent display at UN headquarters.

Imagine that you want to design a guitar with an advertising or promotional meaning, or a "new age" guitar, or a "Boston Red Sox" guitar. How would you do it while keeping it classy? Is *"classy"* the best adjective to describe the message or the impact we want to cause?

A metaphor can be conveyed using different attributes of the design. A message can be expressed (in growing order of obviousness) as: lines and shapes, symbols and logos, words, abstract and figurative painted motifs, carved figurative motifs, and real objects attached to the instrument. In general, abstract elements are more subtle, figurative ones are more obvious.

---

[5] *Exception: the use of bone or fossil materials for the nut. More on chapter 13.*

[6] *Invented word, formed by "escopeta" and "guitarra" (Spanish for "shotgun" and "guitar").*

[8] *So please, no SpongeBob SquarePants stickers, under no circumstances.*

Checklist:

Channeling inspiration

These principles are the best companions for your inspiration:

- **Think "original"**: reinvented, reinterpreted, improved, or just totally out of the box.

- **Use symmetry**. Not only across the main instrument's axis: consider also diagonals and transversal lines.

- **Use asymmetry,** if possible enhancing *function* at the same time (a shorter lower horn introduces asymmetry and may improve balance in the guitar)**.**

- **Keep the lines pure**. Watch the flow of the lines; especially in sharp curves, sudden changes in direction, protrusions (the guitar's horns), and deep concavities.

- **Make it abstract** (in the "shape of a guitar") if you want to achieve originality; make it in the shape of something else if that contributes to the objective of your design.

- Unless you are working with naturally colored, highly figured wood, use color, which is indeed powerful—a pink Strat makes a very different statement than a red one.

- **Use contrast**. Less, when trying to give a more uniform character to the design; more, when willing to "enrich" the design.

- **Use decoration with sobriety**; avoid excess. [8]

- **Be conscious of the message** that is being sent through associations.

- **If the guitar will have a theme, think about different ways of conveying the metaphor.** Remember: figurative elements (pictures, letters) will cause a much more intense impact than subtle, abstract ones (like lines and shapes). *More* doesn't mean *better*.

Frank Lloyd Wright, American architect and writer, said: *"Form follows function–that has been misunderstood. Form and function should be one, joined in a spiritual union."* Such magic happens when our design meets the three objectives of guitar design: **Beauty, Playability,** and **Sound.**

(Photo: Courtesy by Paul Vallejo)

THE TRINITY OF GUITAR DESIGN:

BEAUTY, PLAYABILITY, AND SOUND

- **Objectives of guitar design**
- **Factors of guitar design**
- **Priorities in guitar design**
- **Guitar shape and guitar sound**
- **Defining the instrument of your dreams**

Necessity may be the mother of invention, but play is certainly the father.

-Roger von Oech

The basics

Objectives of good guitar design

A well-designed guitar has to be pretty, it has to feel right when you play it, and it has to sound good.

But a *great* guitar has to be beautiful, it has to feel like a glove in your hands, and it has to sound fantastic.

Ambitious? Of course. Would you demand anything less from your dream guitar?

Beauty, Playability, and **Sound** form three sets into which I have placed several *factors of design* we can work on. Note that these are not goals, nor characteristics, nor attributes of design, but concrete elements under our control: objects, shapes, technologies, accessories, and materials we will deal with.

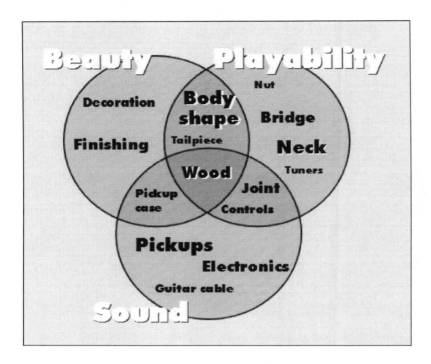

Factors of guitar design

The main factor in **Playability** is *Neck* (including the fretboard). The other decisive playability factor is the instrument's setup, which doesn't belong to the guitar design phase.

Finishing might influence the sound of an electric guitar, but then I cannot identify a particular finish just by ear. By ear, I could say if the pickups are any good, or if the instrument sustains well, though. So, *Pickups* and neck *Joint* belong to the **Sound** set.

Note the difference made between *Controls* and *Electronics*. The *controls* are our interface with the instrument's behavior (volume, tone, balance, etc.); *Electronics* is the technology that physically implements that behavior (potentiometers, switches, cables, etc.).

All components influence the a*esthetics* somewhat, but just a few of them are included in the **Beauty** set: having nice-looking parts is more a purchasing decision than a design one. The **Beauty** set is reserved for those factors that respond to our own creativity.

Would you have arranged those factors differently? Sure, why not. Far from being a dogma, the chart is intended only as a sort of mind map.

The ubiquitous factor: wood

Have you noticed something interesting? There is only one factor that affects all three parameters: *wood*. Its figure adds to the **Beauty** set, its stiffness contributes to a better sustain (and thus, to **Playability**), and its density affects **Sound**. But the wood factor shouldn't be considered a panacea: its contribution is only relative. All factors are important (the font size reveals their approximate relative contribution). Any one faulty element would degrade the whole.

In depth

Priorities of guitar design

Different designs reflect different objectives. Some guitars are visually spectacular, like **Ace Frehley's** smoke-shooting Les Paul, or **Gene Simmons'** bass in the shape of an axe. Such designs are intended to make an impact at a show, and need not be so practical in everyday use.

There may be tradeoffs involved in the design of a visually impressive guitar. For example, **Steve Vai's** heart-shaped guitar cannot be light: it's enormous; therefore it is likely to be heavy. Unless it is made from an extremely light wood, in which case it might be prone to break or twist. Or unless it is made from a superlight space-age material, in which case there's no way it's going to be cheap. And so on.

Other instruments put *ergonomics* first. Their shapes are... *unusual*, and let's admit it, not always pretty: for those guitars *comfort* is the priority. *Portability* can be a priority, too: it will affect size, and it may demand *ad-hoc* technical resources to fold or dismount the neck.

In short: we can design a guitar by taking any priority as the starting point (weight, materials, cost, etc.) but no matter what we start with, the rest of the design will get conditioned by that initial decision.

The critical design factor: body shape

Of all the design factors in the chart, though, *"Body shape"* emerges as the key one:

- Almost any design bias we introduce will translate into a body shape variation.
- The body shape is the very identity of an instrument. A Les Paul is a Les Paul because it has *that* shape and not some other.
- Virtually all parts are attached to the body; the finishing and the main decorative elements, too. In headless instruments, even the tuners.

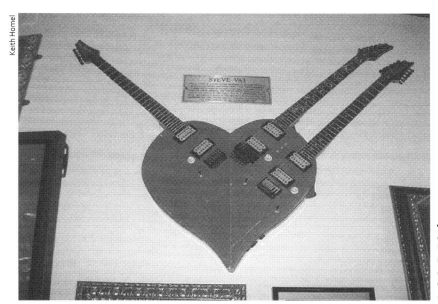

Keith Homel

Just imagine the kind of case this instrument would need! (Steve Vai's heart-shaped guitar, at the Orlando Hard-Rock Café)

- Ergonomics depends on the body shape.
- The body shape emphasizes the musician's personality and visibility.
- Freedom in body shape design is what makes electric guitar design so interesting.
- The body shape is the factor that reflects the designer the most.

What is "good guitar sound"?

Some human sensations are easily expressed with words: I say "dark red" or "olive green" and you know what I am talking about. The same with tactile experiences: *hot, smooth, cold*, etc., and the same with auditory sensations of pitch and loudness, even when not all of us have an absolute ear (*"yep, that's was a loud C Minor. I think."*)

When it comes to *describing* sounds though, things are not that easy. We use words borrowed from other senses: *warm, brittle, high, low, dry, clear...* So let's try to put a guitar's sound into words, as objectively as possible. An ideal sounding guitar (electric or otherwise) should offer:

- **Power**. Volume, projection, amplitude. In electric guitars this is more related to the amplification device than to the instrument itself.
- **Broad dynamic response**. The relative presence of the fundamental frequency and its overtones; a single string is plucked, but the instrument responds as a whole.
- **Variety**. Can you play blues and rock, jazz and classical, just by adjusting the controls (and maybe your attitude)?
- **Responsiveness:** how quickly the guitar acoustically responds to the player's actions.
- **Sustain**: discussed in chapter 12, it is how long a string remains vibrating after it is plucked.
- **Timbre:** the qualities of the sound that allows us to differentiate between a violin and a flute, even though they are playing the same note. It is the perception of the sound at a subjective level, a synthesis of all the physical components of the sound—its very *identity*.
- **Personality**: a recognizable timbre makes a recognizable guitar. Sound personality comes from the associations created between a sound and a given instrument.
- **Evenness:** all strings produce a coherent response in terms of the rest of the parameters.

Does the shape affect the sound?

In the documentary *The Mystery of the Stradivarius*, acoustic physicist **Andrea Iorio** from Cremona, Italy, explains:

> Can one hear the shape of the violin in the sound? If you play a skin-covered drum, can you hear if the drum is round, or some other shape? It took ten years to solve this problem scientifically. And the answer is "no". You cannot, by analyzing the sound –interpreting its quality subjectively– reconstruct the origin and the shape of the instrument.

Two instruments with different shape can produce sounds that are virtually identical; and two instruments with the same shape can sound very different. The very idea of a violin with some unique, ideal shape simply makes no sense. Now, do you believe that the sound of an electric guitar, which sound is produced electro-magnetically, has anything to do at all with its shape? The immediate answer would be "no way". Not even with the most advanced technology.

Granted, the comments above deal with a regression (*from sound to shape*), not a causality (*from shape to sound*). But even if the shape influences sound somehow, other factors will have a far bigger impact.

I used to think that getting a good sound from a guitar was a matter of buying the best pickups available. Now I believe that is only half true. The sound of a guitar depends on many factors. A good pickup will transfer a good sound, just like a good microphone will transfer the voice of a good singer. But if the singer is not so good, then not even the best mic in the world will change that.

Factors that influence sound on an electric guitar or bass

Apart from the pickups, many other factors will influence the sound of a solid body instrument (in no particular order):

- **The amplifier you are using.** Its technology (tubes? Solid state?), its quality, its settings... and a long *et cetera*.
- **The effects you are using**. Guitar effects are precisely designed to alter the signal, and consequently, the sound.
- **Resistance of the circuit.** Number of pots in the circuit, their values, their wiring, etc.
- **Capacitance of the circuit**. How many capacitors are present? Which values do they have? How are they connected?
- **The setting of the pots**: the sound –not only the volume– may change depending on the pot being set at maximum, or not!
- **Construction type and quality.** Which type of neck joint does the guitar have? Are the bridge and the nut slots well made? Etc.
- **Quality, gauge and condition of the strings.**
- **Quality and length of the cable.**
- **Stiffness and density of the wood.** Is it made of brittle, thin, hard maple, or soft, thick, dense, "creamy" mahogany?
- **Material of the frets**–or the absence of them.
- **Body.** How massive is it? How thick it is it?
- **Size of the cavities in the body.** The hollow spaces inside the guitar's body can introduce a "semi-acoustic" character to the sound.
- **Setup.** Are there buzzes? Are the strings too close to the pickups?

The list certainly doesn't end there. But we will discuss many of these factors (and some others) in the next... 180 pages.

Checklist

Defining the guitar of your dreams

At this point, you only need to be aware of these considerations–we will convert them into design decisions later on:

- **Think about the scope of your instrument.** For example: it is going to be used for practice, for performance, or for both? What kind of performance?

- **Which style of music will be played with that instrument?** Heavy metal? Klezmer? Blues? Or will the guitar be used to play a little bit of everything?

Which characteristics are vital to this particular design? These are some options:

- **Beauty** is the typical focus of *stage*, commemorative, or collectible instruments. If that is what you are trying to design, **Part II** of this book **("Beauty")** will be especially interesting for you.

- **Playability**, *sine qua non* condition for those who happen to value the *touch and feel* of a guitar above everything else. If this sounds like you, focus on **Part III - Playability**.

- **Sound**, the "pot of gold at the end of the rainbow" for those who put music first. **Part IV - Sound** is for you.

- **Cost.** How important is this variable to your design? "Most expensive" does not always mean "best", but good quality will impact cost–"cost" here is understood not only in terms of money, but as an investment of time and effort, too. **Part V–Parts, Materials and Finishing** contains some interesting ideas plus considerations about ecology, wood selection, and finishing options.

- **Portability.** For people who travel a lot, an easy-to-carry instrument is not a small advantage. Weight, size, shape, and materials will have to be carefully chosen.

- **"All of them!"** So, you want to create a new classic... Okay, enjoy *everything* that comes next!

Part II

<u>Beauty</u>

4: Design of the body shape (2D: The outline)

Character, identity, ergonomics... all come together in the guitar's body. Designing its shape is perhaps the most fundamental part of developing a new instrument. In this chapter we will review the dimensional attributes of beauty, and how to apply them to the body's shape.

5: Design of the headstock

The headstock shape is influenced by the number and distribution of the tuners, and the aesthetic conception of the instrument. In this chapter we will review some structural characteristics (angle and joint), as well.

The essence of the visual personality of a guitar: the body shape.

Photo courtesy of Dieter Stork.
Instrument: Lospennato Radiostar www.lospennato.com.

DESIGN OF THE BODY SHAPE
(2D: THE OUTLINE)

- **How to design classics, how to design radicals**
- **Templates and guides for guitar design**
- **The guitar body: 2D considerations**
- **2D prototyping**

"She has curves in places where other women don't even have places."

– Anonymous

The guitar body: 2D considerations

How to design classics, how to design radicals

Creativity is a spark, but the initial ideas need time to decant, to take definitive shape. Let's give our ideas a spectrum of possibilities, so they have enough room to find their own path. The following chart depicts electric guitar and bass body shapes using two axes: **Convexity/concavity** and **straightness/curvature** of lines. Categorized in this way the bodies go from *curvy* to *pointy*, and from *minimalistic* to *convoluted*.

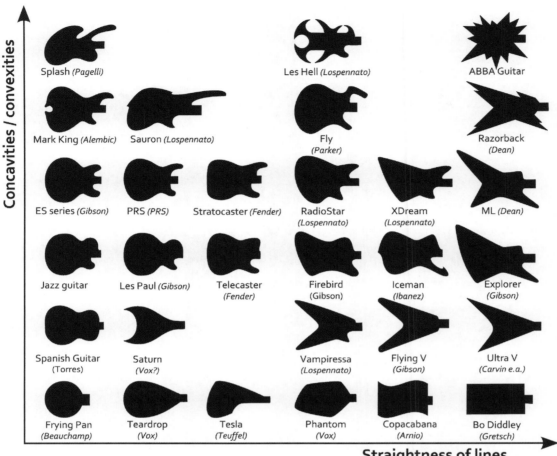

The chart axes are labeled: vertical axis "Concavities / convexities" and horizontal axis "Straightness of lines". The guitar shapes shown are:

- Splash (Pagelli)
- Les Hell (Lospennato)
- ABBA Guitar
- Mark King (Alembic)
- Sauron (Lospennato)
- Fly (Parker)
- Razorback (Dean)
- ES series (Gibson)
- PRS (PRS)
- Stratocaster (Fender)
- RadioStar (Lospennato)
- XDream (Lospennato)
- ML (Dean)
- Jazz guitar
- Les Paul (Gibson)
- Telecaster (Fender)
- Firebird (Gibson)
- Iceman (Ibanez)
- Explorer (Gibson)
- Spanish Guitar (Torres)
- Saturn (Vox?)
- Vampiressa (Lospennato)
- Flying V (Gibson)
- Ultra V (Carvin e.a.)
- Frying Pan (Beauchamp)
- Teardrop (Vox)
- Tesla (Teuffel)
- Phantom (Vox)
- Copacabana (Arnio)
- Bo Diddley (Gretsch)

The more extreme those variables get, the more radical the instrument looks. A lot of concavities, or none. A lot of curves, or none. That is how a radical design emerges. But find a balance of curves, draw a conservative number of concavities, and the more "traditional" the body will look. That is why the classic models are closer to the center of the chart, and the radical ones are closer to the borders (the Spanish guitar qualifies as "radical" here, because it is out of context: an *electric* guitar with that shape would be radical indeed!)

This chart is not exhaustive—on the contrary, each shape represents several others. Counter-examples can be found, of course. For example, just attach the neck on the wrong end of a Stratocaster, and you get a radical guitar with the exact same concavity/straightness combination as a Strat.

Here's another thing about extreme body shapes. Extreme body shapes are usually *unergonomic*—the instruments at the top-right of the chart don't look comfortable to play and probably aren't. The biggest offender is the "ABBA guitar", which represents the maximum value in both scales. The designer surely decided that these new kids from Sweden needed some visual impact to have a fair shot at the 1974 Eurovision Contest. [9]

---

[9] *Their costume's designer probably thought the same thing. It worked, anyway: ABBA won the contest that year.*

The first draft

I prefer to start by drawing the lower-left bout (the place where the player rests the arm). There is no particular reason for that. Then I continue with a light contour to define the body, which I will erase and redraw a hundred times, here and there, until I come up with a pleasant and balanced whole. This phase should not be encumbered with too many rational considerations—just let the pencil flow, instead. Start over again, as many times as necessary. This is the moment to be creative. I spend a lot of time designing body shapes for two reasons: First, it's my favorite part of the process. Second, I am an obsessive perfectionist about it; I keep making changes so subtle that not even a microbiologist wielding an electron microscope would notice. My only consolation is to know that for a luthier perfectionism is not entirely a bad thing.

Design templates: a thousand-year wisdom

There are no recipes for generating beauty, but some attributes of beauty (symmetry, proportion, equilibrium, etc.), are of a dimensional nature, so we can make use of some geometrical, referential frameworks to base our creative process.

The Vesica Piscis

Literally meaning "the bladder of the fish" in Latin, the *Vesica Piscis* is a symbol considered sacred in ancient times. It is made from two circles of the same radius, intersecting in such a way that the center of each circle lies on the circumference of the other. It evokes very strong associations, and it is therefore natural that ancient instrument makers searched to attain perfection in their designs by basing them on such a "perfect" figure. The intersection was considered an image of the contacting worlds of Earth and Heaven, matter and spirit. It is a symbol of completeness. It also symbolizes a fish, a secret paleo-Christian symbol, representing Christ and the saints. This shape has been not only used in the design of stringed musical instruments, but also in architecture around the world. It is said to have been used to design violins and instruments that have a "teardrop" shape, like lutes. It is the most basic of layout tools, but it can help our perception of symmetry, balance and proportion when designing the body .

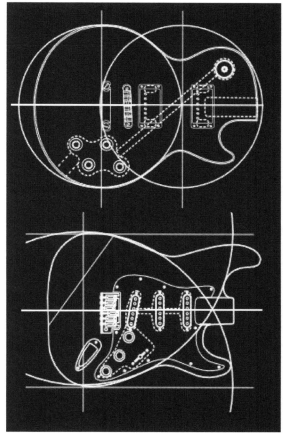

Would it be useful to design an electric guitar? Yes—at least as a first approach.

Were the LP and the Strat designed using this resource? Can't say for sure—but look how well they fit in those curves! Note also that in one case the Vesica is used vertically, and in the other one, horizontally.

The Golden Ratio

Made popular through the bestselling novel *The Da Vinci Code*, the Golden Ratio is a design resource used for millennia (literally), since ancient Greece times. It describes a relation between two segments, one of which is 1.618 times larger than the other one. This relation is found in an astonishing number of instances in nature, clearly more frequently than pure chance would suggest. So, a guitar designed using this principle would be perceived as consistent with proportions found in nature and also in culture. See in the figures below how well the LP and the Strat fit in the golden rectangle. Look at the position of the bridge in the Les Paul, and at the precise golden relation between the width at the upper bout and the length of the Stratocaster body.

Was it deliberate? Did the designers of the classics use the golden ratio as a guide? I don't know. I made a test with a few bodies of my own design (also shown below) and they too fit in interesting ways to these proportions–*but I did not use the Golden Ratio as a basis for those designs!*

The golden ratio can be used as a first, basic guide to design the body. It can be used simultaneously with the Vesica Piscis, too.

$$a + b$$

$$\varphi = \frac{a + b}{a} = \frac{a}{b} = \frac{1 + sqr(5)}{2}$$

(or: **a+b** *is to* **a**, *as* **a** *is to* **b**)

$$\varphi = 1.6180339887...$$

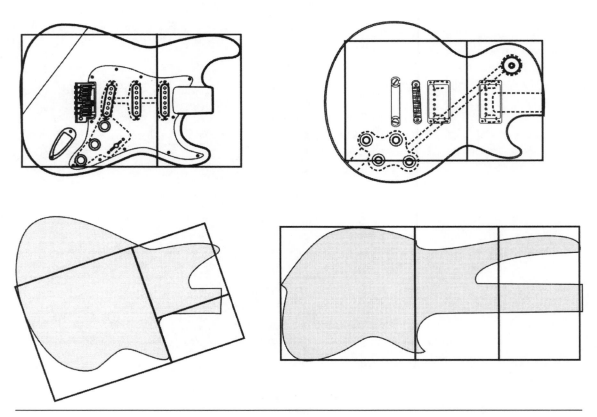

The "gitarrendesign" template

Unlike the previous examples, this is a template specifically adapted to guitar design. Inscribing the body and the headstock within the delimited zones will assure that both elements will be in proportion with each other. The dotted lines propose good places for the guitar's waist, and the limits of the upper and lower horn and/or cutaways (see figure on the right).

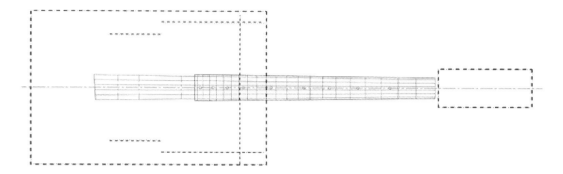

Note how the upper horn line coincides with the 12th fret, which is a good rule of thumb to achieve a balanced instrument (see chapter 6 - Ergonomics). This template is available for free in the downloads section of www.gitarrendesign.de (website in both German and English).

Horn insertion lines

I want to introduce you to a design trick that, in my experience, is useful to improve visual harmony. Take, for example, the following body shapes, in which the lines of the horns have been extended through the body or neck.

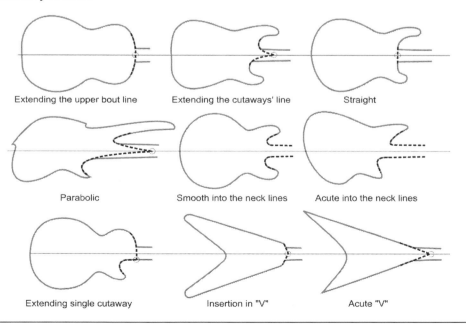

Extending the upper bout line	Extending the cutaways' line	Straight
Parabolic	Smooth into the neck lines	Acute into the neck lines
Extending single cutaway	Insertion in "V"	Acute "V"

Notice how the horns do not just stick out from the body, but are a continuation of the upper bout and/or the cutaways. The extended lines converge, or stay parallel, or interact in some other way that makes sense, giving *continuity* to the design. I omitted "bad" examples on purpose—in such cases, the shape of the body looks "disconnected" somehow.

Another benefit of this horn insertion line approach is that the shape of the heel will be easier to integrate with the rest of the design. If the horns follow very divergent paths, it will be more difficult to make them meet in the back of the instrument.

2D prototypes

Prototyping is a process that I highly recommend during the design phase. Even if the "prototype" is just a simple cardboard cut in the shape of your guitar's body:

- It will save costs, by preserving the materials that will be used on the real instrument.
- It will help to test the body shape from an "ergonomics-based" perspective (you can anticipate the look and feel of the real thing, testing how comfortably the model fits in your body, simulating your hands access to controls and higher frets, etc.)
- You can adjust the body's size, if necessary (just stand with it in front of a mirror with it).

Checklist

Designing a great guitar body

- **Use templates to ensure good proportions**, but do not constrain your designs too much by them.
- **Reinventing the classics.** If you want to use a known model as a reference (for example, if you want to re-create an Explorer, or design a stylized Jaguar) using a real size drawing of the original as reference will ensure that your design has a compatible size. Also, by knowing where the original curves lay, you can find new paths for your own lines. You can get real size plans from several providers on the internet, or just draw the outline of a body using a real instrument.
- **Use more than one drawing medium,** if you have to. Pencil and computer complement each other.
- **Prototype!** Cut a cardboard or plywood silhouette of the body, and simulate playing on it standing up, sitting down, etc. Does it look comfortable? How does it fit on your knee? Would you be able to reach the whole fretboard? Now is the time to make all necessary adjustments.
- **Let it mature.** Hang the draft on a wall where you can see it from your bed, your sofa or your desk. One day you notice a curve that needs to be corrected. Do it. Then after another few days you may notice that the upper horn angle is a little off. Correct it. Always keep the original drawing somewhere, though, so you can appreciate the evolution, or even start again from scratch.

The process continues until a few days pass, and you can't (or won't) make any more changes. **That is the outline of your new guitar body.**

*A pretty unusual headstock shape
in this Kay bass.*

(Photo courtesy www.harvesterguitars.com)

5 HEADSTOCK DESIGN

(OR THE COMPLETE LACK THEREOF)

- **Function of the headstock**
- **Headstock shapes, size and angle**
- **Tuners placement**
- **Branding elements: logo and truss rod cover design**

[SPOON BOY] (After bending a spoon with his mind): *"Do not try and bend the spoon. That's impossible. Instead, only try to realize the truth."*

[NEO]: *"What truth?"*

[SPOON BOY]: *"There is no spoon."*

[NEO]: *"There is no spoon?"*

[SPOON BOY]: *"Then you'll see, that it is not the spoon that bends: it is only yourself. "*

—from **"The Matrix", film by L. & A. Wachowski, USA, 1999**

The basics

Function of the headstock

The headstock (also called "peg head", or just "head") fulfills two main functions.

- One is structural: it serves as support for the tuning machines.
- The other is aesthetical. The design of the headstock is almost as important as the design of the guitar body.

Once again, the classics will serve us as reference to compare two completely different (but equally valid) design approaches.

Stratocasters feature a headstock that accommodates the tuners in a "6-in-line" configuration, as opposed to the Les Paul's "3+3". The Strat headstock shape has become a classic, and many guitars produced in the decades following that instrument's introduction have a similar shape, or a variation of it.

The Strat's head has no angle with respect to the neck shaft, which is a departure not only from previous electric guitar models, but from practically all other stringed instruments (in lutes, for example, the headstock is angled back 90°). Such design favors mass production, as whole necks can be machined from a single piece of wood, on a single machine and with little waste. Necks with angled headstocks must either be cut from a large billet of wood, leaving a large piece of waste wood behind, or they are made from two pieces glued together, a more lengthy manufacturing process.

A Stratocaster's headstock resembles a 2D rendition of a violin's pegbox and scroll, an idea used in some guitars from the late 1800s. It is original, simple, pleasant to the eye, with positive associations, and one of the most recognizable items of the brand. It's all a good headstock must be.

In contrast to that of the Strat, the headstock of the Les Paul is angled back and accommodates the tuning machines on both sides, sticking to more traditional designs. The top line of the LP headstock outline has the famous "open book" (or "moustache") shape, a design copyrighted by Gibson which led to a lawsuit against Ibanez some decades ago.

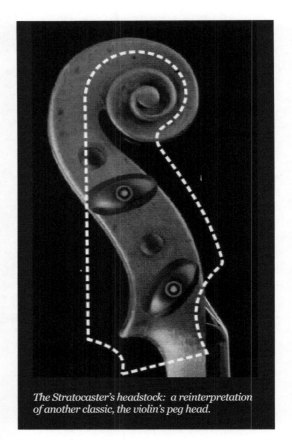

The Stratocaster's headstock: a reinterpretation of another classic, the violin's peg head.

Headstock shapes

Some manufacturers use the same headstock shape for all their instruments. This is efficient from a production point of view, and contributes to brand identity: you see that headstock and you recognize the brand. The price paid for this strategy though, is to give up on visual character of the individual instruments in the line. Guitars intended for different musical genres (country, rock, metal, semi-acoustics, signature models) all of them have the same headstock, which generally has a neutral shape (examples in the figure on the right: Warwick and Framus). I use only one headstock shape for my instruments, too, because I build only a few models, all in the same style.

A counter-example is Gibson: Les Pauls, Firebirds, Flying V's, etc. each have their own headstock shape, and in all cases the design of the headstock complements the visuals of the rest of the instrument (second row in the figure).

The headstock must be in aesthetic harmony with the body shape. Les Pauls feature a headstock that has no common lines with the body, but which is nonetheless a nice match: the head is as elegant as the body. The Flying V takes a different approach. It has a head in a "V" shape, which reinforces and echoes the radical "V" shape of the guitar–visually, this works great too.

Which headstock shapes are the most radical? The ones with the most (or the least) concavities and straight lines, of course! Parker's have a headstock that can be considered minimalist. It has only enough wood to support the tuners, and little else. The design is elegant and modern. It might not be as sturdy as a full-sized headstock, and it could break more easily if the instrument fell badly, but those guitars are extremely light, which reduces that risk.

Headstock dimensions:

- **Size:** Design it in proportion with the rest of the instrument, not too big or too small.
- **Length**. The whole instrument should not be longer than 39" (990 mm), to avoid problems locating a big enough case or gig bag; the maximum headstock length must be decided in concert with that of the rest of the instrument (which, by the way, is a practical proportionality check). The headstock must be big enough to mount all the tuning machines, of course. More on this in a bit.
- **Thickness**: 5⁄8" (about 16 mm, give or take 1 mm for the finishing) is a pretty standard thickness, adequate for most tuning machines.

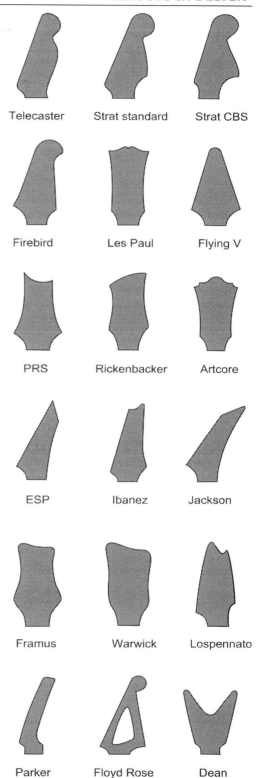

Telecaster Strat standard Strat CBS

Firebird Les Paul Flying V

PRS Rickenbacker Artcore

ESP Ibanez Jackson

Framus Warwick Lospennato

Parker Floyd Rose Dean

53

Headstock angle

The Les Paul headstock is at a 13° angle to the neck shaft. The greater the headstock angle, the greater the breakover angle of the strings at the nut. And the greater the breakover angle of the strings the more firmly they sit in the nut slots. This can have a positive effect on sustain.

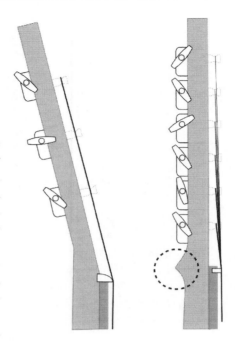

An angled headstock also makes the strings lay on the same plane when viewed from the side. In the figure, compare how the strings are disposed on a Les Paul's headstock, with all strings on a plane, vs. on a Strat head, where each string has a different angle. In the case of the Fender style headstock, string retainers are usually needed for some strings to increase breakover angle, so they can sit more tightly in the nut.

A headstock angle of between 13° and 15° is more than adequate. Angled headstocks do exist with as little as 11° and as much as 17° of angle, but these extremes are not that common. There is a trade-off that involves *vulnerability,* though: angled headstocks tend to break more easily, both due to bad falls or when the guitar lies on its back:

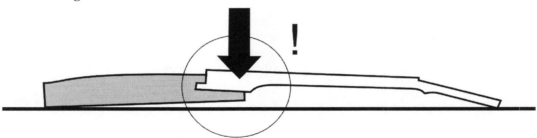

One way to increase strength at the headstock joint is carving a volute under it (from the Latin *voluta,* "scroll"–see it highlighted in a circle on the fender neck on the figure at the top). The volute adds mass to the head/neck joint. It is said that it reduces oscillations, improving sustain, too. But the main benefit is to reduce the chance of breaking the neck at the nut, not uncommon in heavy guitars, like Les Pauls (which don't have a volute). But keep in mind that they are not universally used. It takes more work to build a neck with a volute, some folks just don't like the look, and some players complain that they get in the way of their thumb when playing in first position. As with all design decisions, all factors should be considered when deciding whether or not to use a volute.

Worst case scenario*: The recipe for a vulnerable neck would be a long headstock with 6 tuners in line, a strong angle, no volute, all attached to a thin neck and a very heavy body.*

Standard guitar headstock angles:

0°: All Fender models - 4°: Guild - 13°: Peavey and Warmoth - 14°: Gibson Firebird, Explorer, Washburn, most budget Epiphone replicas of Gibson models - 17°: Gibson ES-335, Les Paul, SG

Standard bass headstock angles:

0°: All Fender models - 10°: all Gibson basses - 12°: Yamaha SBV - 14°: Epiphone

Headstock joint

Fender's headstock (0° angle) is just a prolongation of the neck. Angled headstocks are often *joined* to the neck, instead (see picture). An angled head made from one piece of wood has increased risk of breakage (see top figure on the left), as the short grain at the headstock makes it vulnerable.

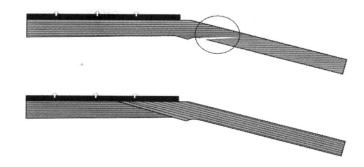

The second neck shows the headstock joined to the neck using a **scarf joint**. The grain lines running parallel to the face of the headstock make it much more resistant to shock. Also, note how the wood piece that forms the headstock also defines the volute.

Strings headstock path

The *headstock path* of each string is **the segment of the string that runs from the nut to its tuner**. The strings' headstock paths on a Les Paul are **non-parallel**: they separate in two divergent groups at the nut. A divergent path will give you more freedom to design the shape you want, but it can put the nut under unnecessary stress. Divergent string paths can also cause some problems if the angles are too severe: the greater the angle, the more sideways force is exerted by the string on the wall of the nut slot. This can tend to make the strings pop out of the nut slot.

In a Stratocaster, on the contrary, the strings stay parallel after they go past the nut. To design a headstock in such style you must define the position of the tuners first, and develop the shape of the headstock as a function of the resulting distribution. This will limit the shape the headstock can have, though, forcing a pointy, more or less *triangular* shape.

For the perfectionists out there: Take into account the different thicknesses of the strings when defining the exact placement of the tuners, if you want to ensure *perfect* string parallelism.

Different paths of the strings from nut to tuners: divergent in Les Pauls, parallel in Stratocasters.

In depth

Tuner placement

1) Distribution

If you have a headstock shape in mind already, simply find the best distribution you can, regarding tuners and other elements.

On the contrary, if you want to design the headstock from scratch with its *function* as the main priority (leaving the shape for later), you have to make two decisions:

The first decision regards tuner distribution (3+3? 6-in-line? 4+2? etc.); it can be done according to your preference or the style of the guitar.

- **3+3 (2+2** in basses) goes well with conservative, classic guitars (jazz, country, single-cutaway bodies, and semi-acoustics).

- **In-line** tuners can work better on more modern guitars, since the head-stock will end up having a longer, more stylized shape.

- Other combinations are possible (like the **4+2** combination—**3+1** in basses) of course. But be aware that you'll have to buy the tuning machines individually, that is, not as a set (they come in both left side and right side configurations).

Give the tuners enough distance from each other, so they do not interfere. The precise distance will depend on the tuning machines design. Les Paul's tuners are placed about 1 9/16" (40 mm) from each other. Stratocaster tuners are located 1" (25.4 mm) from each other, *measured from post center to post center*, which is about as close as you can practically place them.

The second decision regards the strings' headstock paths, as discussed above.

2) Position.

As seen in the figure on next page, the tuners have to be correctly placed in relation to the edge of the headstock. This demands taking careful measuments both of the tuner machines and the headstock, to ensure that the holes are drilled at the correct distance from the edge.

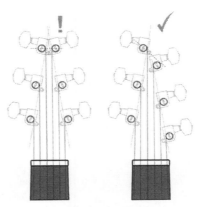

3+3, parallel string path. *The top two tuners won't fit together. The left group or the right group has to be moved an inch or so.*

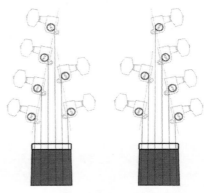

4+2, parallel string path. *Modern look, used by MusicMan. The 2+4 distribution (right) is possible, but not usual.*

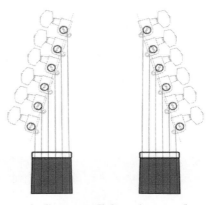

6-in-line–parallel string path.. *The tuners are closer to each other. The reverse option (on the right) was popular for shredders' superstrats.*

No headstock at all!

In the 80s, American luthier and designer **Ned Steinberger** (read interview with him at the end of this book) developed a radical concept on electric guitars and basses: instead of the headstock, the strings got anchored on a metallic headpiece, and the tuners were built into the instrument's bridge. These instruments, which perfectly matched the *Zeitgeist* of that decade, quickly became popular–and they still are!

If you build a headless guitar, you may expect the following: [10]

- The instrument will almost certainly have good balance.

- The construction will be easier (no head joint, no angles or volutes).

- The special hardware required will be, on average, more expensive than regular bridge and tuners.

Avoid the low quality headless parts you can buy for a few bucks on eBay. Go for real good ones. Check `www.abm-mueller.de`.

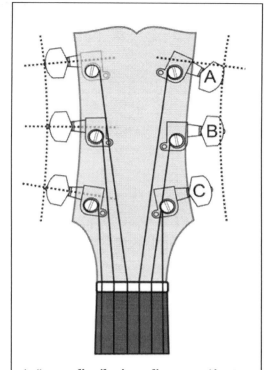

A "3+3" distribution, divergent (the Les Paul's way). The tuners on the left are placed correctly, perpendicular to the curvature of the headstock's edge.

The other tuners are placed incorrectly:

A: It is non perpendicular to the edge (sometimes seen in basses, though–needed for a better reach).

B: The tuner is too close to the edge.

C: the tuner is too far from the edge, interfering with the adjacent string.

Other headstock's elements

Truss rod cover

As we will see later in chapter 7 ("Neck design"), the neck straightness and *relief* (a subtle upward curvature) can be set by adjusting the truss rod, a metallic piece that runs along the inside of the neck. One of the possible accesses to the truss rod adjustment nut is through a cavity routed in the headstock. This cavity is normally covered by a–not surprisingly–so called "truss rod cover", which is fastened with small screws. The truss rod cover must be big enough to serve its purpose, but not as big as to impact placement of the tuning machines. You can simply buy a truss rod adjusting nut cover. But the truss rod cover presents another opportunity to add personality to the design. It is also a good place for your logo.

---

[10] *Apart from some 80's-related jokes you might suffer because of it...*

Logo

A logo is a graphic mark or emblem used for identification and recognition of a brand or manufacturer. Logos are either purely graphic (symbols/icons) or include the name of the person or organization, in which case is sometimes called a *logotype*.

Logos can be inlayed (as in many Gibson instruments), or applied in the form of a decal (Fender style), or carved into the wood. I have my logo laser cut from a thin metal sheet, and glued to the instrument before the transparent finishing coats are applied.

Take a look at the following logos, and try to identify some common characteristics:

Did you notice?

1) Almost all of them are based on surnames.

2) They use *script* fonts, that is, typographies that resemble handwriting.

3) Most of them are slightly angled, imitating a signature.

4) Almost half of them include the word "guitars".

Probably the first idea that will arise in your mind will be that of using your own name as your brand and/or logo, and that is perfectly okay. If you want to design a logo in the same traditional style than the ones above, then your job is half done: find a script font you like, write your own name with it, add some graphic elements (an artsy underline, a variation in the initial letter or some other character), and there you go. If you want to design a more original logo, though, you can either hire an expert consultant or try yourself. But, be aware that logo design is a complex discipline, a subject of study in itself, full of aesthetic, artistic, psychological and symbolic connotations; it needs a lot of dedication and experience to create logos that can be considered "great", or even "good".

The following link points to an article on the Internet, *10 tips on how to avoid common mistakes in logo design*. The first point on the list is "having your logo designed by an amateur", be that you, a friend, or an inexperienced graphic designer.

```
http://www.smashingmagazine.com/2009/06/25/10-common-mistakes-in-logo-design/
```

But if you really want to design your own logo, check the following website, which lists "45 Rules for Creating a Great Logo Design":

```
http://tannerchristensen.com/rules-for-logo-design/
```

From my part, I wish to offer these "dos and don'ts" of logo design, with focus in guitar branding:

Do, if possible	Avoid, if possible
▪ Are your guitars "heavy metal"? Vintage-like? Futuristic? Design the logo in a style that mirrors that of your instruments. ▪ Ideally, make the logo recognizable both vertically and horizontally (the positions in which a guitar is normally held or looked at). ▪ Make it timeless. Ignore current trends. For example, as I write this, one of the latest *hips* in logo design is using a *lot* of colors! ▪ Design a *memorable* logo: easy to understand, easy to remember, easy to recognize, and different from the rest. This is the main challenge of good logo design. ▪ Ignore the rules, if you must (even these ones).	▪ Guitar branding *clichés*—for example: guitar outlines, 6 lines representing strings, G clefs, etc. ▪ Copying others. Not only names (tough luck if your last name happens to be "Gibson"!), but also fonts, graphic elements, etc. ▪ Designing too complicated a logo. It might result confusing to understand, details may get lost, and it will be difficult to carve, inlay, etc. ▪ Using too many fonts (more than two), or too complex ones. Trying to read the logo will result difficult, even annoying. ▪ Diffuse, "ghostly" outlines, timid presence, gradient colors. Always go for a clear, solid visual statement.

If you don't have a logo and don't want to invest time or money in getting one, just use your signature. It doesn't have to be your real signature, especially if your penmanship is like your doctor's. You could use a simplified, stylized version instead. It looks elegant, and it is very simple to make: just use a permanent marker.

Be aware, though, that if you apply solvent-based finishing coats *after* the signature, the solvents may ruin it. This is where a truss rod cover comes in handy: you sign on it, and if something goes wrong you can always build another one.

Checklist

How to design a great headstock

Neck / headstock joint:

- **Unless you want to design a Gibson-style neck, include a volute** under the headstock joint to reinforce the headstock joint.

- Remember that a heavy body can make the neck/head joint vulnerable.

- If you are designing a 12-string guitar, it is a good idea to reduce the neck angle, to compensate for the extra headstock length.

Tuner placement:

- Place the tuning machines not too close to, not too far from, and always perpendicular to the headstock's edge.

- For guitar tuning machines, calculate a distance of at least 1", measured *from post to post* (that is *not* 1" *in between* tuners!) In basses, for example a Fender Jazz Bass, this distance increases to 1 7/8" (47.6 mm) between posts. In other words: These are the distances *from hole center to hole center* on the headstock's front. Before drilling, check that this is enough room for the particular tuning machines that you plan to use!

Originality / personality:

- **Keep it simple and elegant.** Avoid, if possible, shapes that are copies of other headstocks. Put your personal touch in it.

- **Style.** Design a headstock that reflects, or visually complements the body shape. Contrasts in shape work too, but achieving a body-headstock visual harmony will be trickier in such cases.

- **Design your own truss-rod cover.**

- **If you use stamped serial numbers,** the *back* of the headstock is a good place to stamp them.

- **Put your logo on it,** or your signature. Do not leave your guitar unidentified. It should carry the name of its maker.

Tim Patterson

Truss rod cover in the shape of the Empire State Building (note the little biplane flying around the skyscraper!)

Part III

Playability

6: Electric guitar ergonomics

In this chapter we identify the limitations of conventional guitars and basses regarding a correct interaction with the player's body, and the way to overcome that legacy. We will also see how the body's geometry, and in particular the upper horn, determines if the instrument will stay in a correct playing position when the instrument is played while standing up.

7: Neck design

In this chapter we will analyze the influence of the neck back shape, angle, and other dimensions on the playing experience.

8: Fretboard design

In this chapter we will discuss the influence of the fretboard's geometry on intonation, actions, sustain, etc. Perhaps the most technical chapter of them all, but the one with the biggest influence on the final quality of your design.

Billy Beale and his 1959 Hollow-Body Harmony Meteor Guitar. Reaching the high frets? No problem!

(Photo courtesy: Phil Palmer–Kansas City , Missouri)

6 ELECTRIC GUITAR ERGONOMICS

- **Ergonomics while playing standing and seated**
- **How to design a body with great balance**
- **The guitar body: 3d considerations**
- **3D prototypes**

Sure you got the looks... but have you got the touch?
Don't get me wrong—yeah, I think you're alright
But that won't keep me warm in the middle of the night...

—"That Don't Impress Me Much",
Shania Twain, Mercury Records, 1998

Ergonomics–A definition

The term *ergonomics* is derived from the Greek words *ergon* [work] and *nomos* [natural laws] and it has been around since the 19th century. The central concepts of ergonomics though, appear to have been applied already in ancient Greece (5th century BC), where they used ergonomic principles in the design of their tools, jobs, and workplaces.

So, we can define ergonomics as *the scientific discipline concerned with the interactions among humans and other elements of a system (activities, workplace, equipment), the goal of which is to improve well-being and overall system performance.*

We can identify the following objectives of ergonomics:

- **To increase safety;** in the short term, but mostly in the long term, in the form of the prevention of repetitive strain injuries.

- **To increase ease of use:** ease of access, ease of operation, easier interaction.

- **To increase comfort,** preventing stress and tiredness in the human part of the system.

Guitar ergonomics

When we say "human part of the system" we are referring of course to the player; the guitar is the other part, a very interesting one from an ergonomic point of view. A guitar is not like a machine we operate from a distance, like a TV-set: both bodies (man and machine) are in contact, they "vibrate" together.

Ergonomics in guitar making is not new; traditional stringed instruments have had many ergonomic features for centuries. Examples are the rounded back shape of the neck, the waist of the acoustic body (which allows resting the instrument on the player's leg when playing seated) and the angle of the neck in the case of instruments of the violin family and arch top guitars.

Electric guitars and basses include even more ergonomic features. Examples are the tummy bevel and the arm rest of the Stratocaster (comfort), the cutaways of the guitar body (ease of access to the upper frets), the radiused fretboards (performance improvement), finger rests, rounded-over fret ends, and the strap we use while playing standing.

The guitar body: 3D considerations

Until now we have considered the guitar's body from a "2D" standpoint (its outline). The next paragraphs will start the review of the guitar body as a volume, which is the dimensional characteristic with most impact on ergonomics.

The guitar top

The top surface of a guitar's body normally adopts one of these shapes (see figure on next page):

- **Flat top.** Like a Stratocaster.

- **Cylindrical top.** The body will have a variable thickness, like for example the Yamaha RGX series.

- **Arched top.** The carving will adapt to the edges of the body, like on a Les Paul, hollow body jazz guitars, some Superstrats, and many others. The irregularity emerges as a natural geometrical consequence of keeping the body thickness constant at the edge and arching the top, like a violin.

- **Decorative top**. A figurative or abstract motif is carved in the wood.

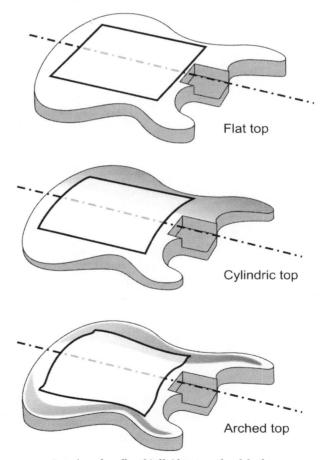

Flat top

Cylindric top

Arched top

Imagine a handkerchief laid on top of each body.

A "beauty-related" comment: Carved bodies can have more visual impact than flat ones, especially on instruments with high-gloss finish. Have you noticed how, for example, Les Pauls seem to be glossier than Strats? That is because the arched Les Pauls top will reflect the light rays in multiple directions, while the flat surface of a Stratocaster will reflect light in only one angle at a time.

The guitar's body edges

Rounded-over edges, like those in a Stratocaster, are more ergonomic. The human body relates more comfortably to them than to sharp edges (like in a Les Paul).

But again: rounded-over edges are not compatible with binding or with carved tops in general. Use them with flat tops.

The radius of the Stratocaster edges is approximately ½" (12.7 mm). The radius of the Les Paul perimetral edges are ca. 3/32" (2-3 mm) on the front, and 5/32" (4mm) on the edge of the back.

Ergonomics while playing standing

This section is about the ergonomics of the guitar when it is played standing up, hung from your shoulder on a strap. The key factor in this case is *balance*, an elemental, but vital precondition for good playability.

Have you ever played a "neck-heavy" bass, or one of those guitars that tend to point to the floor? The neck of a neck heavy instrument must be supported by the fretting hand. This can increase fatigue in that hand. Some say that a slippery nylon strap can be the problem, so they recommend using wide leather straps with shoulder pads. *What's next, avoiding silk shirts?*

There is nothing wrong with the strap. The problem is the guitar. It's out of balance, as a consequence of the geometry of the body shape.

The guitar's headstock is the number one suspect in a "heavy neck" case. The worst scenario is a bass with six, seven, or more strings: a lot of large tuners pushing the headstock down from the far end of a long, long neck. But despite the appearances, the headstock is, at most, just an accomplice.

The weight of the guitar's body counterbalances the weight of the headstock, so the trivial solution is to design a guitar with a heavy body. This is the case with Les Pauls: they are usually heavy (they have a thick, massive body), and consequently balance well. But there are design consequences of using body weight alone to maintain good balance. Relying on the guitar's body weight can create other problems, like increased vulnerability of the neck to damage from falls, playing fatigue, etc.

What about a headless guitar? Yes, they can balance well, and oh, I love how they look so much. But if you play jazz, folk, country, blues, or other traditional genres, you may want to use a guitar that doesn't look like it was taken from a Duran Duran video clip. [11]

As in classic murder stories, the culprit of the neck-diving crime is the one that you may least suspect. **The key to the balance of a guitar is the location of the upper strap button,** which is defined by the length of the upper horn. After all, the guitar is hanging from that point; that is the very fulcrum of the instrument. The following graphic shows a guitar in playing position, hanging from the strap. Notice the balance axis drawn from the strap button down.

---

[11] *There you go: an 80's-related joke.*

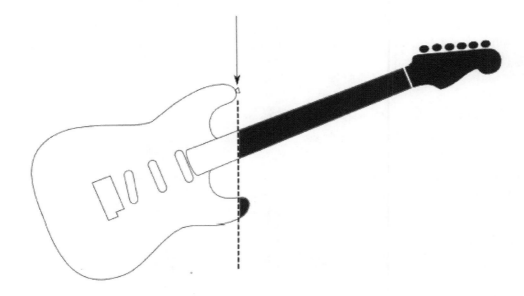

In short, the guitar will balance better or worse depending which "half" has more leverage. The darker parts are the ones weighing the headstock down. In the case of Stratocasters (which balance well) the white part weighs slightly more than the dark part–which is a good thing.

Please notice that "weighs" here is used in a rather simple minded, graphical fashion, because we really must consider leverage, too. Weight differences near the balance point will have little overall effect on balance while small differences in weight at the extreme distances from the balance point (the tail end of the guitar and the headstock) can have a major effect.

What would happen with guitars of other shapes? Let's see how a Firebird balances. Because it has virtually no upper horn, the guitar hangs from a point too far away from the headstock. The "dark side" is much bigger.

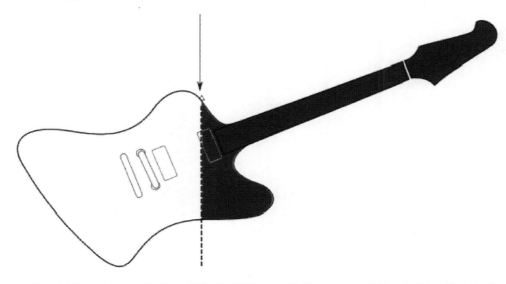

And look at the *lower* horn. One would not think of the *lower* horn as having anything to do with balance, right? Well, it does, as long as it has become a big chunk of wood added to the dark side. Note that the neck pickup is also on the dark side of the figure and will add to the imbalance. The problem would be more noticeable in basses, because of the increased leverage of a longer neck–the Thunderbird (which is the "bass version" of the Firebird) being one of the usual suspects when it comes to neck heavy instruments.

Surprise test! How would you improve the balance of the Firebird depicted above (without modifying the body shape)? (Hint: remember the key of balance discussed a few paragraphs above–the solution, in the footnote below [12]).

In the following picture you can see different types of guitar horns (the longest ones being the Strats' ones) with the strap buttons clearly shown:

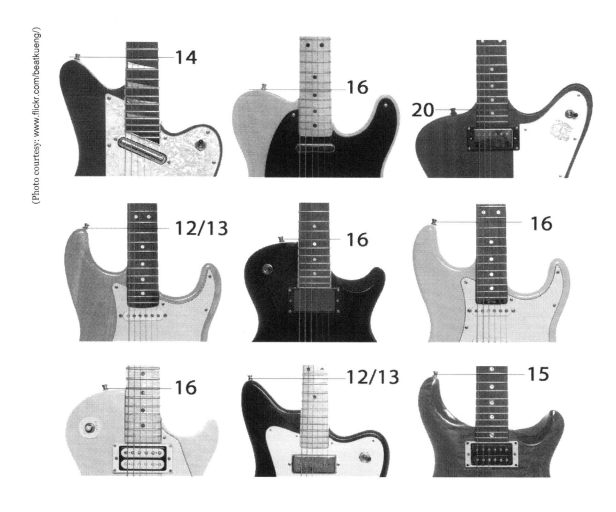

(Photo courtesy: www.flickr.com/beatkueng/)

---

[12] *Answer: Relocating the strap button, of course. A few centimeters closer to the neck will reduce the dark side.*

When designing a guitar for good balance, do not exaggerate the length of the upper horn, though. If the upper horn is excessively long, the instrument might hang offset the player's torso:

Upper horn is too short   Upper horn is too long   Upper horn is just right.

Some guitars and basses have the strap button located at the heel. This may be a good location balance wise for those instruments, but there are ergonomic tradeoffs which should be considered: every time your playing hand needs to reach the higher frets it finds metal, leather, and who-knows-what-else in its way. This doesn't bother all players, but it drives some players crazy.

Ergonomics while playing seated

These graphics show the different ways we hold a guitar while playing seated, highlighting the points of stress on the player's body.

Playing seated. *Torso and guitar lay parallel. The guitar's waist leans on the right leg. Both arms have to adopt forced positions. A "the tail wags the dog" scenario, which eventually causes tiredness in shoulders and arms.*

Changing legs only worsens the situation. The left arm has to extend almost completely to reach the lower frets. The playing hand takes a stressed position, as do the shoulders.

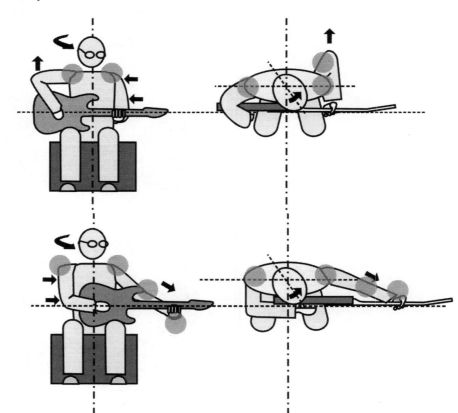

Inclining the instrument improves things for the left arm, but the shoulders stay uncomfortable. The whole playing arm has to be hold in the air.

Rotating the torso relaxes the right arm, since now it doesn't have to go around the guitar body so much. However, the player's waist is twisted, and the legs have to adapt, too.

***Inclining the guitar instead of the torso is the most common playing position.** But the left shoulder muscles keep the left arm in the air, and the torso will tend to bend over the guitar, after a while.*

*This **should** be the "natural" position, with the instrument slightly inclined (but do you see the catch?)*

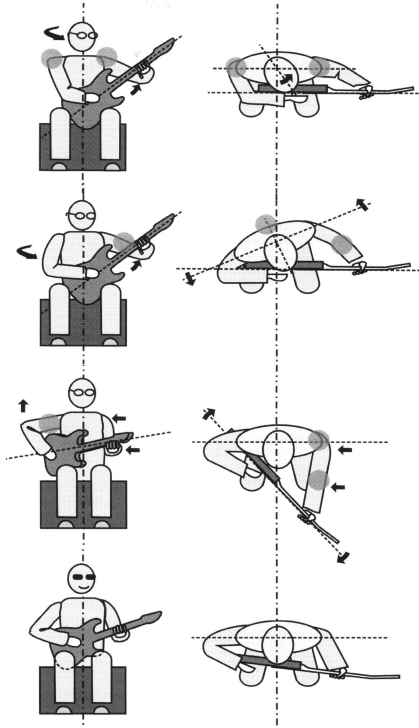

This drawings were inspired by **Rick Toone's** "Dove Hip Hole" video, which you can find on YouTube.com, and are reproduced here with his permission. Rick specializes in ergonomic designs: visit www.ricktoone.com.

There is a problem with the "ideal" position, though (last position on the previous page): it is an impossible one, at least with a conventional electric guitar. The legs and the guitar's body just **overlap.**

The body shape of electric guitars typically emulates the body of Spanish guitars (the "woman" shape, with an upper and a lower bout). But with solid body instruments, where shape and sound are only loosely related, it is possible to build a guitar that will rest comfortably on either leg, and will allow the player to adopt a relaxed seated position, like the prototype shown on the right. But modifications intended to improve ergonomics need to be approached in terms of *design tradeoffs:* a supposedly "ergonomic" feature may create other problems.

Improving ergonomics

How do we know that an ergonomic feature is actually an improvement? First, it has to contribute to one or more of the objectives of ergonomics we listed above (safety, comfort, and ease of use); second, it has to create an overall performance improvement of the "player/guitar system"—preferably on the "player" side of such system.

So, we have to evaluate the impact of the new feature in terms of **playability** (understood as comfort, ease of access) versus the following:

- **Vs. beauty.** As our perception of beauty in a guitar is influenced by the historical models, to design a guitar that is both ergonomic and pleasant to the eye will be a challenge.

- **Vs. ease of operation:** For example, a body recess for the right leg (like the prototype shown in the pictures) would increase comfort, but limit the available room for the guitar's electronics. The controls area may need to be shrunk or relocated.

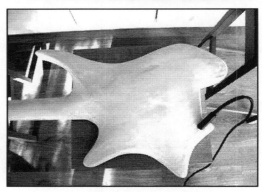

Innovative guitar shape in this prototype designed by Ola Strandberg. The curves fit the legs, the torso, and the playing forearm. Notice the shape of the heel, and the peculiar placement of the cable (guitarworks.thestrandbergs.com).

- **Vs. portability and storage.** Conventional cases, stands and hangers might not work well: An unconventional body shape needs unconventional accessories.

- **Vs. sound.** This applies fundamentally to acoustic instruments, in which the shape of the sound box might impact the acoustical response of the instrument, but the impact on solid body instruments must be considered, too.

➤ **Vs. playability itself.** For example, imagine a modification of the lower cutaway that improves comfort of the knee at expense of a good access to the higher frets.

If your instrument will include any radical ergonomic features, building a prototype will help you anticipate their impact, both positive and negative. Then you can redesign those features accordingly, until you are satisfied with the result.

Then comes the test of time: we can definitively state that something is *ergonomic* only when it has proven itself to be, for long enough time and in different playing situations.

3D prototypes

Using pencil and paper is the simplest way to develop a design, but a simple 2D drawing software can be used as well by those so inclined. Artistic drawing software such as Adobe Illustrator, CorelDraw, Inkscape, etc. will suffice.

Whatever tools you use for making your drawings, there may come a time during the design process when you want a better idea of what the body will look like in three dimensions. 3D drawing software (generally referred to as solid modeling software) can be used for this purpose. Examples of this CAD - "Computer Aided Design") software are AutoCAD, IntelliCAD, TurboCAD, SolidWorks, Alibre Design, or one of the free, open source alternatives.

Using such 3D software would allow for a complete description of the volumes, carvings and cavities. But software of this type requires a high investment of time to learn how to use it, so prototyping using solid modeling software is probably convenient only for those already working with such applications.

A simpler way: 3D modeling using ceramic clay

Despite being familiar with computers, I like to use a simpler and more primitive way to build 3D models: **ceramic clay**. The reason is that you need to know not only how the ergonomic features will look like, but also how will they *feel* like. What we visualize in our minds or on a screen will not always work in the same way on a real 3D object.

A model made out of wood will do, too. I find clay to be more practical, because I can add or remove material, making corrections until I understand how the planes and volumes interact with each other. If necessary, I can start from scratch, or reuse the material for other prototypes in the future.

A 10 kg (22 lb) pack of clay should be enough to build a prototype in real size–but working in a smaller scale saves time and effort. Remember to cover the clay with a nylon sheet between sessions, so it can be reused; otherwise it will solidify.

Checklist

We have described ergonomics improvements as strongly tied to design trade-offs. And such situation is clearly visible in the following points: each line includes the word "*but*"!

- **A longer upper horn may help balance the instrument**, since the upper strap button is located there–*but* not *too* long.

- **The smaller or less protruding the lower horn, the better**, because it adds a little to the dark side. *But* the lower horn has to be big enough as to support the instrument comfortably on the knee while playing seated.

- **Deep cutaways in the lower horn favor balance a bit**, and give better access to the higher frets. *But* a deep cutaway, combined with a horn that serves to lean the instrument on the knee, may result in a long, *thin* lower horn, which makes it susceptible to breaks if the instrument falls.

- **Short upper horn? Compensate with the body.** Models which have no upper horn at all (Explorers, Firebirds, Thunderbirds, for example), compensate the balance with a lower bout that extends a long way back. But if the instrument extends too much, it might result too heavy, depending on the wood you are using. Plus, a matching passing case, stand, and other accessories might be hard to find.

- **Keep the weight under control.** Some guitars will balance well just because the body is really heavy. *But* after playing it standing up for a while, it might feel as if you are holding a bear sleeping on your arms.

- **The smaller/lighter the headstock, the better.** *But* remember: the size and length of the headstock should maintain a harmonic proportion with the body, and be big enough to accommodate the tuners.

- **Go for a flat top** if you want the easiest, most practical option. A carved top can be more fun to make, though.

- **Bevels**: Arm bevel, cutaway bevels, tummy bevels can increase the ergonomics of an instrument. Remember that binding cannot be applied on beveled areas.

- **Did I say already that building a prototype is a good idea?** Use plywood or cardboard to make a small scale version of the instrument. Hang the prototype from a nail set on the place in which the strap button would be, and see how it balances (for this test, model the whole instrument, including neck and headstock). Simulate the use of the guitar in the seated position, placing the prototype on something acting as your knee (a pencil, for example). Improve the lower line of the body as needed.

- And yes, to avoid neck-diving, a good quality strap will work better than a cheap nylon one.

There are some topics yet to be discussed regarding the 3D aspects of the guitar body. They are, among others: the cavities (the internal spaces where the pickups and the electronics are placed), and how to calculate the thickness of the guitar body. But first we have to approach some previous, necessary concepts.

Be patient, young padawan.

(Photo courtesy of Tiagø Ribeiro)

NECK DESIGN

- **Neck back shapes**
- **Neck angle and its relation to the guitar top**
- **Truss rod selection**

"In essence, String Theory describes space and time, matter and energy, gravity and light, indeed all of God's creation, as music."

– Roy H. Williams (author and marketing consultant)

"Aww, come on man... I can barely handle 6 strings!"

Kenny Hickey (guitarist of band "Type o Negative")

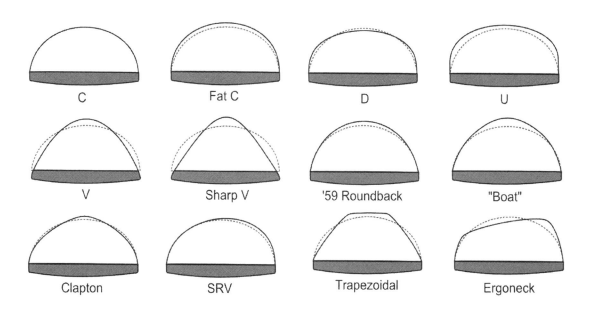

C	Fat C	D	U
V	Sharp V	'59 Roundback	"Boat"
Clapton	SRV	Trapezoidal	Ergoneck

Neck back shapes

Consider the variety neck backshapes shown in the previous page. The *C* shape is the most standard, so it is used as a reference (dotted line) to better appreciate the other shapes.

D, *U* and *V* are some of those other shapes, developed over the years, shown on the chart below. **Sharp V** is a rare, extreme version of the V shape.

I have also included some models offered by neck manufacturer Warmoth: the **'59 Roundback**, the **Clapton**, and the **SRV/"Stevie Ray Vaughan"** model , a slightly assymmetrical neck backshape, subtly different than the **C** shape.

The neck back shape is one of the most influencing factors in playability, and those profiles are a consequence of the evolution of the instrument and the quest for enhanced playability. The *C* shape combines some of the advantages of the rest: it is thin (in comparison with the *U* and *D* shapes, for example) but still has enough girth to serve as a comfortable support for the player's thumb, which doesn't happen with a sharp *V*.

While we are talking about ergonomics, note that the SRV is *asymmetric,* providing more support for the thumb on the bass side of the neck, and less wood on the treble side, to allow a better reach for the fingers.

I have included two pretty radical designs. The **trapezoidal** neck, by **Rick Toone**, and a design of my own, an asymmetrical neck profile (called the *"Ergoneck"*), developed using a left hand in natural "C" position as reference (both models are patent pending).

From a design standpoint, the subject of the neck back shape is relatively simple. You choose the one that your customers (or yourself) prefer, and in case of no special requests, choosing a *C* shape would mean to stay on the safe side of things.

The challenge though, is when it comes time to *build* the neck, particularly regarding *consistency*. Not only consistency of the neck with itself (making a smooth, "bumpless" surface), but also consistency between necks you produce.

Guitarist **John Petrucci**, talking in an interview about the six or seven MusicMan guitars he uses in live performances, singled out one of them. He said that this one guitar provided him with a perfect feeling of security and comfort, because that neck felt special. Now, how it is possible that *one* of the necks felt so special, being an exact replica of the others? When I say "exact replica" I am talking of a *computer-controlled* kind of replica, a matter of a few thousandths of an inch, something clearly beyond human perception.

Who knows–maybe it is a setup thing, or a subjective impression of the player, without any measurable physical counterpart. In any case, the point is: if consistency is perceived subjectively, even when using CNC technology [17], it becomes much more of a challenge when working by hand. The good news for the designer, the luthier and the musician, is that consistency is mainly a problem for companies with a large scale production.

---

[17] *CNC stands for "Computer Numerical Controlled" machines, which are operated by automated programs, as opposed to a human-operated machine.*

Neck angle and its relation to the guitar top

Neck angle is rarely a simple aesthetic choice. The angle of the neck in relation to the body is a function of your choices in regard to the shape of the guitar's top and the bridge hardware you will use. In the arch top guitar, an angled neck is pretty much a requirement, the same way a non-angled neck is a requirement on a flat top instrument.

Once again, Les Pauls and Stratocasters are examples of two different paradigms: LP's have an angled neck (3.5°), and Strats have a straight neck. In both cases, the neck angle is consistent with the geometry of the guitar's top (carved on a Les Paul, flat on the Fender).

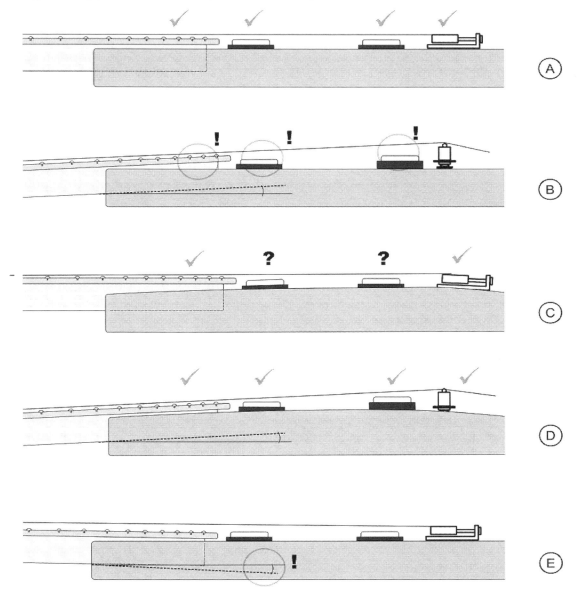

The angle of the neck will influence other aspects of the design, too, particularly the choice of bridge. For the moment, let's look at the different "neck angle / guitar top" configurations:

A - The simplest option: Fender's way. Flat-top or cylindrical-top instruments use a non-angled neck and bridges designed for flat top guitars. The pickups can be mounted directly in the body or pickguard, or on short pickup rings.

B - Inelegant option I: an angled neck on a flat top will produce a lack of parallelism between the neck and the top, but that is the least of your problems: the strings would be placed too high above the pickups. Conventional bridges for flat-top's guitars simply won't work.

C - Inelegant option II: A Neck with no angle on a carved top would not always work in a visually pleasant way. It may be impossible to find suitable bridge hardware and pickup mounting hardware. The strings will come very close to the top or the pickups at the apex of the arch.

D- The Les Paul way. Arch tops fit better with an angled neck. You'll need to use a bridge made for arch top guitars, and the pickups will need to be mounted in high pickup rings.

E - Worst case scenario: A *negative* neck angle. The instrument would be impossible to setup correctly.

Pros and cons of using an angled neck:

Pros	Cons
● Angled necks are perceived as belonging to a more traditional, qualitative making style. ● It brings the head toward the player, which increases playing comfort (see graphic below)	● It is more difficult to build than a straight neck; especially the neck pocket. ● The playing hand may not rest on the guitar's top angle. ● Angled necks are generally glued (as opposed to bolt-on), which makes replacement and repairs more difficult.

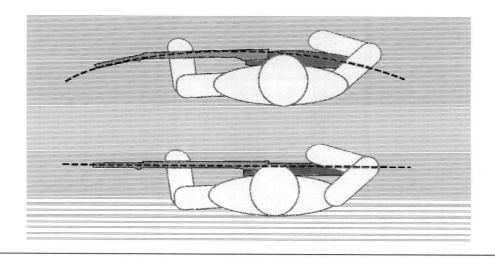

Neck depth

The neck *depth* is the thickness of the neck measured cross-section. In most classic models, this is usually just under 1" (25.4 mm).

One common mistake is to make the neck *too* thin, expecting a "faster" instrument. There are several good reasons to avoid doing this:

- A thinner neck may allow better reach for the fingers, but may increase fatigue of the playing hand.

- In extremely thin necks, the opposite becomes true: fretting becomes difficult; the lack of support for the thumb affects the movement of the playing fingers.

- A thin neck is more vulnerable to twists and breaks.

- A thin neck is more difficult to keep straight. Setting up the instrument will become harder and more frequent.

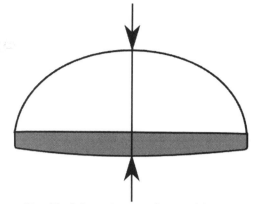

"Depth" of the neck. In modern models it gets smaller as the neck approaches the headstock– not for example on a Telecaster.

The theoretical minimum neck thickness is established by truss rod pocket depth. According to my experience, thicker necks are regaining popularity. It all depends on the player preferences, though.

Standard measurements–Neck depth (at nut and 12- fret)

Les Paul, Explorer, SG: 13/16" and 7/8" (20 and 22 mm); Telecaster: 1" (25.4 along the whole neck); Telecaster deluxe, Stratocaster, Jaguar: 13/16" and 1" (20 and 25.4 mm); Jazz Bass: 29/32" (23 mm along the whole neck).

The truss rod

When I was a 15-year-old kid, holding my first electric guitar (a crappy Les Paul copy, made in who-knows-where, but which I fondly remember), I was told that inside the neck there was something keeping it straight. Daring to adjust the thing was beyond my tender and impressionable mind. Of course, there is nothing mysterious about the truss rod: just something clever.

The truss rod is a long, adjustable steel piece used to stabilize and adjust the lengthwise curvature of the instrument's neck, a critical aspect of playability. The truss rod function is to counteract the string pull, adjusting the neck to stay either straight or *relieved* (slightly curved upwards, as shown in the diagrams in the next pages). A neck equipped with a truss rod will be thinner, more comfortable and more stable, particularly in basses.

In the design phase we are concerned with two things regarding the truss rod: choosing the type, and choosing the point of access for its adjustment.

Truss rod types

These are our options:

- **Adjustable, single action**. If the neck is properly built, a 1-way truss rod is enough to adjust the neck from a perfectly straight neck to a more "relieved" one. The truss rod is fitted in a channel with variable depth routed from the back of the neck, and covered with a wood strip afterwards (see photo below). The shortcoming of this type of truss rod is that they cannot correct an already back bowed neck. Note also that the truss rod channel must follow a curve, which is harder to route (some curved, specially made routing template will be necessary.

Placement:

Action:

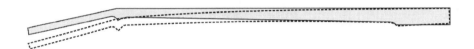

View of the wood strip covering a trussrod channel routed on the back of a neck.

- **Adjustable, dual action**. It can be tensed in either direction. They fit in a channel directly routed into the top of the neck, which later gets hidden under the fretboard.

  Placement: Note how the truss rod channel is easier to make, since it is straight and routed on the top surface on the neck. The fretboard will cover the channel.

Action: The truss rod can *either be loosened* (turning its adjusting nut counterclockwise) which will force the neck to bend upward (up bow), or tensed (turning the adjusting nut clockwise), which will force the neck to bend downward (back bow), lowering the string action.

Lastly, we can name the existence of non-adjustable truss rod. This is basically a rigid rod that keeps the neck straight. Used in steel string guitars during the first half of the 20th century. These are definitely outmoded for electric instruments because of their lack of adjustability. The commercial form of this kind of truss rod is a 3/8" x 3/8" x 14" square steel tube. They are still in use in classic guitar making, but are not recommended at all for electric guitars.

Truss rod adjustment access point

The truss rod adjuster nut can be accessed from different places, depending on the type of truss rod we are using.

A Truss rod **adjustable from the headstock** is easier to access, but it can weaken the headstock joint. If the adjuster nut will be covered by a traditional cover, space for it will have to be provided when laying out tuning machine placement.

Adjustable from the heel: There are two general cases in which this type of truss rod is used.

The first case is for instruments like the Strat where there is over an inch between the end of the neck and the neck pickup. Although Fender s adjustable from the heel traditionally use a slotted adjuster nut and require you to either remove the neck of move the pickguard to get at it, it is possible and common to use spoke nut or Allen nut truss rods and route a small channel into the body to provide access to the nut from the heel end. This is a very common approach, it is easy to access and nothing has to be removed to make adjustments.

The second case is for basses which almost always have a lot of room between the end of the neck and the neck pickup. Either of the above-mentioned heel end schemes can be used here, but because you have so much room to work with you can even use a hex nut adjustment, either under a removable cover or in a short channel wide enough to accommodate a wrench.

So basically the only case where it is not possible to provide simple to use heel end truss rod adjustment is the case where the neck pickup has to be butt up against the end of the neck: In this case you have no choice but to use headstock end adjustment.

Anyway, if you are willing to move the pickup about ¼" back from the end of the fingerboard you can use a "spoke nut" truss rod with heel end adjustment. It is easy to access and nothing has to be removed to make truss rod adjustments.

A truss rod adjustable from the head. No truss rod cover is used.

A truss rod adjustable from the heel.

Truss rod length

Truss rods come in different lengths, 18" for guitars and 24" for basses (including the adjustment nut) are the standard measures. The rod must extend from at least the middle of the first fret at the headstock end to at least into the area of the heel.

The length of truss rod used will depend on which fret the neck joins the body and the scale length, i.e. on the unsupported length of the neck shaft. An 18" truss rod will work well for most guitars, but remember, such standard components might not work on your instrument if you are using an odd scale length.

How many truss rods?

If your guitar has 8 strings or more, or 6 strings or more in the case of basses, you might have to install two truss rods inside the neck. Compensating too much string pull might at some point ruin the nut, or the threaded segment of a single truss rod. Adjusting two truss rods might be more work than working on just one; on the plus side, two truss rods will prevent a wide neck from twisting and will more adequately counteract the string pull.

FRETBOARD DESIGN

- **Main dimensions and geometry**
- **Frets: number, placement, anatomy, selection**
- **Special fretboards**

Do it again on the next verse, and people think you meant it.

-Chet Atkins (American guitarist)

The basics

How many strings?

As you surely know, basses normally have four strings. Five-string basses have become increasingly popular, though, and it is not unusual to see basses with 6, 7 or more strings, normally in the hands of musicians who need them to express all the dimensions of more complex or unconventional musical styles. The number of stings will greatly influence the playing experience, because a wider neck/fingerboard will be necessary to accommodate them.

In guitars, the normal choice is narrowed down to 6, 7, or 12 strings (the latter with 6 courses of 2 strings each). Anything out of the norm means that special parts will be necessary (special strings sets, special pickups, special bridge, special nut, a wider neck, extra tuners, etc.).

Fretboard main dimensions

The neck and the fretboard hold three "secrets": the *touch and feel*, the truss rod, and the key to a good sustain. But let's start from the beginning.

Scale

The fretboard must follow precise dimensions and relations, which cannot be altered without compromising the tuning or even the ability to play at all. They are described in this figure:

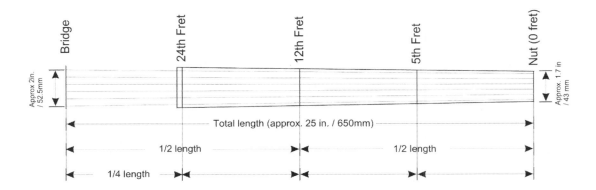

The total vibrating length of the strings (from nut to bridge) is called the **scale** of the instrument, which is the fretboard's main descriptor. The scale determines the precise positioning of the frets, and the *theoretical* location of the nut and the bridge. I say "theoretical" because the *real* location is going to be affected by a necessary "compensation" process.

Which length is better? A long scale will produce, with other parameters kept constant, an instrument with a slightly better sustain. For a given pitch and picking displacement, the longer the string, the more tension it will be under, and the more inertial energy it will have; it will take longer for it to stop vibrating completely. Longer scales have a positive influence on 5 or more-string basses; the additional, thicker strings can sound "flabby" on shorter scale basses. In basses, a longer scale is a natural consequence of the low frequency notes that the instrument is intended to produce. The strings will be stiffer and thicker, which can produce better quality low tones than a thinner gauge.

A shorter scale bass (30" and 32" are common), on the other hand, implies that the spaces between frets are smaller, which makes fingering easier, as you don't need to stretch your fingers that much. The strings on a short scale bass could sometimes feel a little flabby though, but a thicker gauge will reduce this effect. Each player will have their own preference, which will be a function of the length of their fingers or just a matter of playing habits. On the shorter side of the spectrum is the Gibson EB3, with a string length of 30½" (774.7 mm). This was a very popular bass, with a SG-shaped body [19], discontinued in 1979, but still available under the Epiphone brand. Shorter scales are adequate for 4-string basses, and for players with short fingers.

---

[19] *A bass with SG shape = short upper horn = neck diving alarm!*

Standard guitar scales

Different brands use slightly different scale lengths, a differences that doesn't go unnoticed by the discriminating player.

The standard scale of a classical guitar is 25 $^{19}/_{32}$" (650 mm). For solid body guitars and basses, these are the usual scales:

Stratocaster, Telecaster: 25 $^{1}/_{2}$" (647.7 mm); Les Paul, Explorer, SG, CS356: 24 $^{3}/_{4}$" (628.6 mm); Jaguar: 24" (609.6 mm)

Standard bass scales

Fender Jazz Bass: 34" (864 mm), the most common scale in 4-string basses; A 35" scale (889 mm) is considered extra-long, but is becoming more popular especially in 5-string basses (it improves the sound of the fifth string).

Note that the designer can choose any scale length for a guitar, but that basses can only be made with scale lengths of (or very close to) 30", 32", 34" and 35", because bass strings come in four lengths that correspond to these scale lengths. These are short scale (30"), medium scale (32"), long (standard) scale (34") and extra long scale (35").

The reason a bass designer must stick to the standard scales is because the ends of the strings that wrap around the tuning posts are tapered so that they can actually bend around the posts. The wound portion of the lower bass strings are too thick to wind around the posts.

The longest, reasonably available scale is 37" (939.8 mm), but only for hand-made instruments. Unless you have huge hands, you might find such scale very uncomfortable to play on, and very probably you will have to order custom strings. Bass designers are advised to have bass strings on hand before designing an instrument, or have access to bass string length data such as is found at:

http://www.liutaiomottola.com/formulae/bassString.htm

String spread

Spread of the strings at the bridge

The string spread is the distance between the centerlines of the two *outer* strings, in this case measured at the bridge.

The string spread is a function of the **string spacing,** that is, the distance between *adjacent* strings. The spread of the strings on most 6-string bridges falls in the range 2 to 2 $^{1}/_{4}$" (50.8 to 57 mm). The distance between strings–measured from string center to center–is therefore between $^{13}/_{32}$" and $^{7}/_{16}$" (10.3 to 11.1 mm), being (10.5 mm) a pretty common value. In any case, it will depend on the bridge of your choice.

For basses, common spreads at the bridge are as follows:

- 4-strings: 2 $^{1}/_{4}$" (57.15 mm)
- 5-strings: 3" (76.2 mm)
- 6-string: 3 $^{1}/_{4}$" (82.5 mm)

To be sure, consult the specifications of the particular bridge you plan to use. Slap players need enough room between strings to get their fingers between them for "popping".

Bridges are available with adjustable spread. In any case, the string spread will influence the fretboard dimensions (discussion below).

String spread at the nut

At the nut, things get more complicated. The distance between string centers is not constant. If it were, the thicker strings would look too "crowded". The calculation of the string spread and position requires much precision. To obtain a nut with strings correctly spaced, these are the alternatives:

- Use one of the free online calculators, for example:
- `http://www.guitarrasjaen.com`

Use a string spacing rule. Instructive video on:

`http://www.youtube.com/watch?v=w_a8S9TsG6g`

- Buy a nut already slotted that matches you choice of neck width. This doesn't always works as expected for first time builders, though, because making precisely dimensioned fingerboards is pretty hard. It is most probable having to build or find a nut adapted to the neck width you got, not the other way around.

A non-standard neck width (too narrow or too wide) will be incompatible with standard parts; also, the non-standard spread of the strings will mean that they might not lie above the pickup's magnets.

String setback

The "setback" is the distance from each of the outer strings to the fingerboard edges. It must be around $1/8$" (3 mm) at the nut, and a little more (around $5/32$" /4 or 5 mm) at the 12th fret. For the low E-string add $1/32$" (ca. 1 mm) more, to account for the extra string thickness. In basses is still another millimeter or two wider at the nut (around $5/32$" /4 or 5 mm), and ca. $15/64$" (about 6 mm) at the 12th fret.

Width at the nut

To calculate the width of the neck (and fretboard), you need to know/decide the following dimensions beforehand (all discussed above):

A) **The string spread at the nut** (calculated as the distance between the centerlines of the high E and low E strings at the nut)

B) **The string spread at the bridge** (calculated as the distance between the centerlines of the high E and low E strings at the bridge)

C) **The high E string setback** at the nut (setback at the treble side)

D) **The low E string setback** at the nut (setback at the bass side)

E) **The radius** (i.e. the diameter divided by 2) **of the high E string** (G on a bass). For example, if the diameter of the E string is 0.010", the radius is 0.005" (negligible in practice, since you will be working with tolerances bigger that this, anyway).

E') **The radius of the low E string** (E on a 4-string bass, B on a 5 string bass). For example, if the diameter of the guitar's low E string is 0.042", the radius is 0.021" (almost negligible, too, depending on the kind of precision level you are working with).

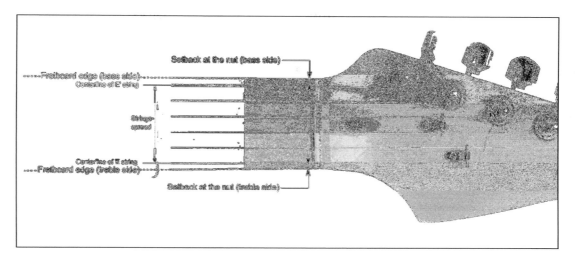

Consequently:

- The width of the fretboard at the nut results from adding: A + C + D + E + E'
- The width of the fretboard (projected!) to the bridge results from adding: B + C + D + E + E'

A straight line connecting both widths (at the nut and the bridge) will define the width of the fretboard along the whole neck. This is when a real-size blueprint of your project becomes indispensable (how to draw an electric guitar blueprint? See chapter 16).

Standard neck widths at the nut for guitars

Fender necks, until 1969, were identified with a letter, to indicate the width at the nut:

- "A" = 1 1/2" (38.1 mm)
- "B" = 1 5/8" (41.275 mm)
- "C" = 1 3/4" (44.45 mm)
- "D" = 1 7/8" (47.625 mm)

Today, the "A" size neck would be too small for a regular size hand. Anything around 1¹¹⁄₁₆" (42 or 43 mm) is the most common nut width. For players with bigger hands, something closer to the "C" or "D" sizes could result in more comfort.

Standard neck widths at the nut: basses

Fender Jazz Bass: 1 1/2" (38.1 mm), Fender Precision Bass: 1 5/8" (41.275 mm)

5-strings basses are (based on Warmoth measurements): "Medium" = 1 7/8" (47.625 mm), "wide" 2 3/16" (55.5 mm)

Frets

Fretted or fretless?

A perfectly valid question if we are talking about basses; traditional double-basses (the biggest instruments in the violin family) are mostly fretless. A fretless instrument feels different and sounds different.

The pressed string is anchored between your finger and the wooden fretboard, not over a metallic fret, so sustain and tone are affected. The question loses some meaning when talking about guitars: their sound is not always welcome to unaccustomed ears. The biggest impact of a fretless guitar is noticeable on the playing experience: making quick, precise chord changes on a fretless guitar will require a highly fine-tuned technique.

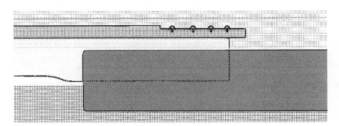

Some fretless basses do actually have frets in the last upper positions, but laying lower on the fretboard. This way, the instruments are capable of producing the sound of a slapped fretted bass when the strings impact on the frets (see figure).

Fretless instruments are easier to build; use harder woods for the fretboard, though, since the friction of the strings is much higher than in a fretted one.

How many frets?

Electric guitars have been built historically with 20, 21, and sometimes 22 frets. The emergence of musical styles technically more demanding and the rise of electric guitar "heroes" have made popular a new style of instrument, very light, very fast, and with 24 frets, which allows a range of two full octaves on each string. The typical examples are the so-called *Superstrat* guitars. For shredding virtuosos, 27 frets are becoming popular. I have seen instruments with as many as 36 frets, but this can be considered an eccentricity. The more frets the instrument has the more difficult it is to set the instrument up to prevent buzzing and the more constraints the designer will have on pickup placement.

Standard measurements–Number of frets

Les Paul, Stratocaster, Explorer, Jaguar and SG: 22 frets. Telecaster, 20 or 21 frets. Gibson and Fender basses: 20. Superstrats, other modern instruments: 24 frets.

Placement of the frets

The location of the frets is calculated as a function of the scale length. Instrument makers have historically used different rules to derive the locations of the frets; these are based on different numeric constants.

In fact, almost nobody calculates fret positions anymore, not even with a spreadsheet; you just use an online fret calculator. Enter the scale length, the number of frets, and *voilà*, you get a complete table of the distances from nut to each fret. Visit for example:

`http://liutaiomottola.com/formulae/fret.htm`

(If you are interested in knowing how fret position calculations are made, keep reading; otherwise just jump to the next topic.)

Calculating the location of a fret is straight forward. If the scale length is 25" (635 mm), to find the distance from nut to fret #1 we have to divide 25/1.05946309 and subtract that result from the scale length, 25. The result is 1 ¼" (35.56 mm)

Where did the "1.05946309..." number come from? **It is an approximation of the twelfth root of 2,** which represents the *frequency ratio* between any two consecutive notes in equal temperament (one "semitone" interval), and since frequency is proportional to string length, that number also represents the length ratio between a tone and its adjacent one–which on a guitar is equivalent to two consecutive frets.

In practice, there is no need to use that number to all of its 8 decimal places. The number 1.05946309 is almost equal to 1.06–the difference is less than a thousandth, by far a smaller error than the ones you will make just by marking those distances with a pencil on a wooden fretboard.

What is important, though, is that the position of fret #2 is calculated again *from the nut*, not from fret #1; otherwise any location errors will compound, which means that by fret #5 or so, those errors could be big enough to affect intonation.

So, in general the equation that generates the distance *(d)* from the nut to each fret is

$$d = S - \left(\frac{S}{\sqrt[12]{2^n}} \right)$$

where *n* is the number of fret you are calculating and *S* is the scale length.

Fretwire anatomy

The width and height of the crown are the variables that identify a particular fretwire type. In a few cases the crown *shape* is a variable, too: It can be semicircular, or "pyramidal" (more *parabolic*, actually). The thickness of the tang is pretty standard, 0.022" (0.55 mm). The barb helps the fret to stay in place in the fret slot.

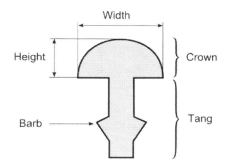

Choosing fretwire

The choice of a particular fretwire type is a matter of personal preference. The best reference is the player's experience: which kind of fretwire did he use in the past? What was the feeling that such fretwire provided? Did the fretwire wear too quickly? Was it hard to fret the notes? (Maybe taller fretwire would alleviate the problem). Did the player note a pitch change in the notes as he fretted the strings harder? (Maybe the frets were *too* high!)

Fretwire selection must consider the following variables:

Fretwire material

Standard fretwire is made of a metallic alloy called **nickel/silver**. The "silver" part refers to the color; the alloy contains no real silver in it. **Brass** was a popular metal used in fretwire. Brass fretwire is still in production, and is used in older instruments. For instruments which need a golden fretwire to match the rest of the hardware, a nickel-free copper alloy is used. **Stainless steel** fretwire has gained some popularity recently. The advantage of using stainless steel is that the frets will last much longer before the instrument needs to be refretted. The disadvantage is that, being a very hard metal, stainless steel is very difficult to work with. Using stainless steel fretwire on a bound fretboard, for example, will require significant work, and nipping off the tang ends will probably blunt your tool's blades.

Playing on stainless steel frets has been described as "playing on ice", because of their hardness. Some say that they produce a brittle tone; I personally find no difference.

Fretwire height

Fret height and string action are closely related. The height of the frets will affect the playing feeling:

- Low frets allow a lower action, making it easier to slide the fingers up and down the fretboard. But the strings will need more pressure from your fingers to fret the notes; plus, bending will be more difficult than on taller frets.

- Frets with a high crown will make it easier to fret the strings. Too much pressure of the fretting fingers can affect pitch though, since the strings stretch as they are pushed down.

Fretwire Width

The width of the fret will affect two things:

- The rate at which they wear. Wider frets last longer, narrow frets wear faster.

- The look: some prefer narrow, vintage-looking frets, some prefer so called "jumbo" frets, very wide and modern-looking.

Fretboard radius

The playing surface of the Spanish guitar's fretboard has no curvature; the strings lay on a common, flat plane. In an electric guitar, the fretboard has a slight curvature, which allows a more comfortable fingering. The strings follow that curvature somehow, and share a tapering, cylindrical surface.

This gives us the opportunity to review a subtle problem regarding the fretboard and its relation to the strings. It's the problem of the **ideal string *action*** (the height of the strings over the fretboard), a critical playability factor. The problem with radiused (cambered) fretboards is that they describe a *cylindrical* surface. But the strings don't follow a cylindrical surface: they follow a *conical* one. The strings don't share a common plane in space–*just like the Ikebana flowers, remember?*

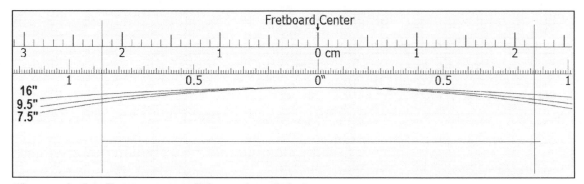

Three typical radiuses, compared (image is real size).

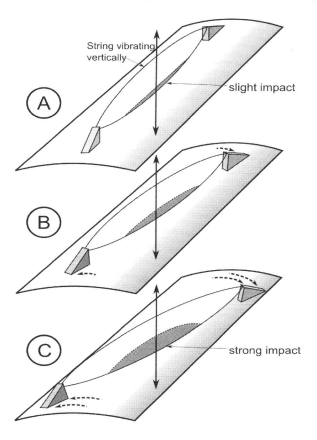

String vibrating vertically

slight impact

A

B

C

strong impact

Consequently, the surface of the fretboard and the "surface" described by the strings are not parallel to each other. This limits how low the action can be set.[20]

Question: If the nut and the bridge have both the same radius, why don't the strings describe a cylindrical surface? They are positioned along the surface of a cylinder with a constant radius, right?

Answer: *No.* Even if nut and bridge have the same radius, the strings lie on *diverging paths* from one another: they don't lie on the *generating lines* of a cylinder. They describe a *longer* path, *closer to the fretboard at the center*, thus requiring higher action to avoid buzzes.

Some modern fretboards are produced with a **conical radius playing surface**, sometimes called a "compound radius" which offer a more curved surface at the nut (so the fretting of chords is easy and comfortable), and a gradually flatter surface towards the higher positions. Such geometry keeps the strings at a constant height from the fretboard, because both surfaces (the fretboard's surface and the imaginary surface formed by the strings) are conical, and consequently, can be (ideally) parallel. Another benefit of a compound radius fretboard is that longer string bends can be done before the string "notes out": as we bend the strings on a curved surface, sooner or later their trajectory will cause them to contact a higher fret, and they will stop producing sound.

In the previous page graphic, a string is seen vibrating above a cylindrical surface (constant-radius). In **figure A**, the string runs exactly parallel to the fretboard. The vertical amplitude is exaggerated, to highlight the effect. The string impacts slightly on the fretboard (thin dark grey zone). In **figure B**, the string runs not parallel, but at an angle to the fretboard. The anchoring points (nut and bridge) are both now on a lower point than before, *down to each side of the curved surface*. So the impact area is bigger, even if the anchoring points have the same height than before, and the vibration amplitude stays the same.

Figure C goes further. The string runs at an even sharper diagonal to the cylindrical surface—just as happens with the high and low E strings in a guitar. The anchoring points lie even lower than before down along each side of the curve, so the string gets closer to the fretboard, in the middle. Note that the impact area is much deeper. That is the reason why in constant radius fretboards it is necessary to keep

---

[20] *Dear, geeky reader with a flair for geometry: please note that I refer here to "cylinders" and "cones" liberally, as simplifying idealizations.*

the action relatively high: to avoid buzzes, especially in the outer strings. A compound radius fretboard minimizes this problem.

Conical (compound) radius fretboards

The next graphic shows the geometry of the different kinds of fretboards. First, the fretboard of a Spanish guitar, which is flat. Second, a cylindrical, constant radius fretboard. Third, a composed-radius fretboard (conical surface). Lastly, the worst case scenario: a compound-radius fretboard which radius doesn't change smoothly: the strings will never run parallel to the fretboard.

Building a compound-radius fretboard with a perfectly gradual change by hand is not an easy thing. It requires the use of a special sanding technique, and practice. Plus, it will never be as precise as a CNC-

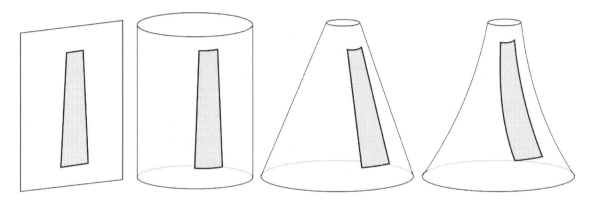

produced fretboard: is one of those things in lutherie that machines do better, faster, and cheaper.

Guitar virtuosos like **Joe Satriani** assert that a multi-radius guitar is nothing short of indispensable for the music styles they play. However, according to researchers in this area (Mottola, Jaen, etc.) putting numbers to the differences between cylindrical and conical section fretboards shows that they are so small as to fall within the tolerances of competent fretwork.

Standard radiuses

In ascending order of radius (descending order of curvature):

Vintage Stratocaster	7.25" (184.1 mm)
Modern Stratocaster	9.5" (241 mm)
Most guitars with LSR roller nuts	9.5" to 10" (241 mm to 254 mm)
Most guitars with Floyd Rose bridge	10" (254 mm)
PRS (Regular)	10" (254 mm)
Warmoth necks	Compound, from 10" (nut) to 16" (heel)
Les Paul	12" (305 mm)
Ibanez	12" (305 mm)
Jackson (newer models)	Compound, from 12" (nut) to 16" (heel).
Jackson	16" (406 mm)

Compound radius is sometimes called "multi-radius", which creates misunderstandings as some guitar brands, Ibanez for example, use the word "multi-radius" in reference to the curvature of the *back of the neck,* not the fretboard. A multi-radius neck is a reproduction of the back shape of famous musicians' guitar necks, copied using digital 3D-scans and CNC machinery. But unless stated otherwise, the fretboard is not multi-radius, but it has a constant curvature all along.

Special fretboards

Scalloped fretboards

Scalloped fretboards have the space between the frets "scooped out", creating a "U" shape. This way, the fretted strings touch the frets, but not the fretboard itself.

It can improve playing speed and makes it easier to bend the strings. It requires practice, though: too much pressure and the guitar will play out of tune; too little pressure and there will be no sustain. Building a scalloped fretboard requires patience and precision. Some instruments are scalloped only in the higher fret positions–the last four, in the Ibanez JEM models, for example, or **Billy Sheehan's** Yamaha bass.

Multi-scale ("fanned") fretboards

Also called fanned fret fretboards, these fretboards use a different scale for each string, creating a non-parallel arrangement of the frets. The use of this feature on electric guitars is attributed to luthier **Ralph Novak** (read interview with him at the end of this book), who patented the fanned fret name and the technique. The reported benefits are that

- The lower strings get a longer vibrating length, improving generation of low frequency tones; the higher strings, conversely, have shorter length and generate a sound more adapted to their frequency range.

- It can favor a homogenous tension across the different strings, improving the "feel" of the instrument.

Checklist

How to build a neck for great playability

- **Be precise when drawing the blueprint.** The most critical precision issues in a musical instrument have to do with the fretboard.

- **Scale, string spread, type of bridge, type of nut, fretboard dimensions, and fret angle:** all have to be decided simultaneously, because they are strongly interdependent (more on chapter 13–"Selecting the right hardware").

- **Use compound radius fretboards.** They allow a lower string action, reduce buzzes, and enhance playability.

- **Design 24-fret instruments,** unless required otherwise.

- **Fret height.** Tall frets will provide more sustain, shallow frets will allow lower action. The customer is the king, let him decide.

- **Fret material.** Go for high quality, hard materials.

- **Invest time in the back shape of the neck.** Take into account the player's preference, hand size, and other such factors. Discuss expectations with your customer.

What is the radius of this fretboard?
What kind of truss rod has it got?
What is the shape of the top?
The twisting of the neck is of course deliberate. An example of bold innovation by luthier Jerome Little.
(www.littleguitaworks.com)

(Photo courtesy Jerome Little, www.littleguitarworks.com)

Part IV - Sound

9: Selecting, placing and matching pickups

Pickups are the most influential elements of a guitar's sound. This chapter gives useful advice on how to choose, match and place the pickups on an electric guitar or bass.

10: Control design

This chapter deals with the design of the "interface" between player and his instrument, resolving a flexibility/simplicity tradeoff. It is about deciding the quantity, type and placement of the controls of your guitar or bass.

11: Guitar and bass electronics

Once the controls have been defined, they have to be implemented electronically. This chapter shows some classic circuits, plus how to connect the different components so you can develop a circuit for your particular needs.

12: Secrets of sustain

One of the most valued attributes of a guitar's sound is the ability of *sustaining* the sound. In this chapter we will review the design factors that keep those strings vibrating–plus some advice regarding construction and setup.

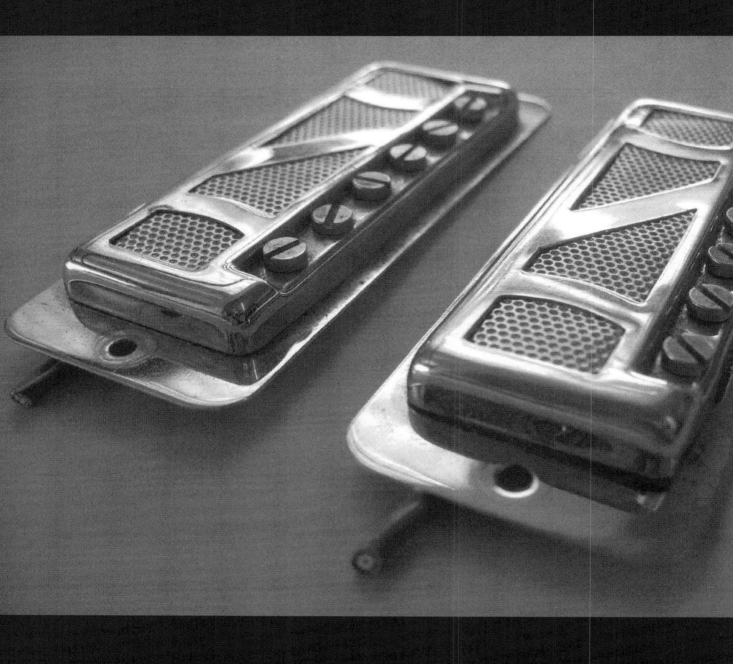

9

SELECTING, PLACING AND MATCHING
PICKUPS

- **Pickups parts and working principle**
- **Resonant frequency of a pickup**
- **Response of a good pickup and response of an inferior one**
- **Matching different types of pickups**
- **Pickup placement and its influence on the sound**

"I seem to have lost my phone number. Can I have yours?"

—**"Pickup"** line from **www.becomeaplayer.com**

The basics

How do pickups work?

The job of a pickup is to convert the vibration of the strings into an electrical signal. The formal name is "transducer", but that term is not in common use.

In its most basic form, a pickup is a magnet with a wire coiled around it. As the strings interact with the magnetic field, the magnet *induces* a proportional electric voltage in the coil. Magnets and coils are the elements that define at the most basic level the sound delivered by a pickup.

Magnets and their influence on the sound

Magnets have different magnetic power, depending on several factors: material, size, remnant magnetic charge, condition (i.e., it is new or old? Has it been subjected to strong magnetic fields? Etc.) But in essence they can be considered to be either *strong magnets* ("hard") or *weak* magnets ("soft").

The stronger the magnet, the "harder" the sound. The signal delivered is stronger. There is a practical limitation though: very strong magnets kill the strings' vibration, the very phenomenon they are supposed to sense.

In severe cases, this magnetic string capture can cause "false harmonics". or "double notes".

Coils influence on the sound

A coil is simply a wound conductor. Its influence on the sound depends on the mate-

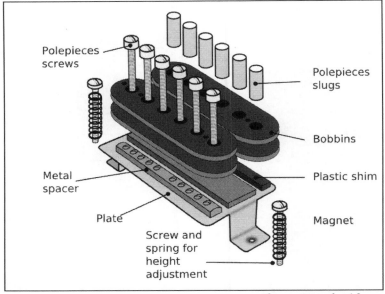

The anatomy of a pickup.

rial of the wire (normally copper), its gauge, its number of turns, the coil's size and shape, and its proximity to the magnets. In electric guitar pickups the gauge is pretty standard:

- **42-AWG** ("American Wire Gauge") is used in humbuckers, Strat pickups, and Tele bridge pickups. It is an ultra-thin copper wire (diameter: 0.0025"/0.064 mm)

- **43-AWG wire** is used in the Telecaster neck position and in Rickenbacker pickups. It requires less turns to attain desired coil values, because it is even thinner: 0.0022" (0.056 mm).

The more turns the coil has, the higher the output will be, particularly in the midrange frequencies. There are limitations in this case, too. An over wound pickup (or too thin a wire) will cause:

- **Loss of high frequencies**, which produces a "muddy" sound.

- **Higher impedance,** also resulting in treble loss.

The coil also affects the sound depending on its condition. A tightly wound coil will have different inductance than a loosely wound one, thus affecting the sound.

It is also imperative that the wire has continuity and a proper insulation (you can't see it, but the wire has a transparent layer of an insulating lacquer. Any scrap will take it off and short circuit the coil).

Standard coil turn numbers

Gibson's PAF Humbucker: 5000–5050 turns per coil. P-90 single coil: 10,000 turns. Vintage Strats (from the 50's & early 60's): 7900-8350 turns. Late 60's & 70's Strats: 7600 -7700 turns.

Interaction between magnet and coil

There are four basic combinations of magnet and coil types, and descriptions of the sound generally ascribed to each. These combinations are used for illustration only; pickups are designed with these extreme characteristics only rarely.

- **Weak magnet + small coil:** sweet, bell-like clear tones. Very low output.
- **Strong magnet + small coil:** glassy, hot Strat sound.
- **Weak magnet + big coil:** smooth, buttery midrange.
- **Strong magnet + big coil:** crunch and rawness. Very high output.

A *small* coil is one with low inductance/impedance—that is, with relatively few turns and relatively thick wire. A *big* coil is one with a lot of winding and a thinner wire—so "small" and "big" do not *necessarily* refer to the physical dimensions of the coil, just the number of turns.

Humbucking pickups

Humbucking pickups are dual coil pickups, constructed in a way that any induced electrical noise (hum) from nearby electrical devices is greatly reduced. Humbucker construction and operation involves two separate parameters: the orientation of the permanent magnets in each coil, and the direction of wind in each coil. Humbucking pickups attenuate induced hum by common mode rejection, due to the fact that the two coils are wound in opposite directions and their magnets are also oriented as polar opposites as well.

The string motion induces current in both coils in the same direction, since the reverse winding and reversed magnet of one coil creates a signal in the same direction as the other coil. Electromagnetic interference (coming from electrical appliances, motors, etc) on the other hand, induces current in *opposing* directions in each coil because it is only sensitive to the winding direction, which is reversed for one coil.

The reason the pickup senses string vibration is because the permanent magnets are oriented north up in one coil and north down in the other, so signals induced by perturbations of the pickup's magnetic fields are *in* phase, and so do not cancel. The noise is cancelled due to *destructive* interference, while the actual signal is increased due to *constructive* interference, thus dramatically improving the signal-to-noise ratio.

Magnets, coils, polarities... Is it really that complicated? Isn't there **one** clear parameter that might help us to anticipate (or to plan for) sound quality? Yes, there is. I invite you to read the following article by **Helmuth Lemme** to learn about it.

The Secrets of Electric Guitar Pickups *

There are lengthy discussions between musicians about the advantages and disadvantages of different pickup models, and for someone who has no knowledge of electronics, the subject may seem to be very complicated. Electrically, though, pickups are fairly easy to understand, so this article will examine the relation between electrical characteristics and sound.

** Reproduced here by courtesy of **Helmuth E. W. Lemme**, author of "Elektrogitarren– Technik und Sound", and other books on guitars electronic and amplification. The first complete version of this article was published on "Electronic Musician", December 1986, p. 66-72. This article has been shortened and edited by the author of this book to make it more relevant to the design phase of an electric guitar or bass. The complete version can be found on:*
http://buildyourguitar.com/resources/lemme/

[25] *Example: "Cathedral" by Van Halen.*

I am sorry to say that most pickup manufacturers spread misleading information about their products, in order to drive sales. So some factual corrections are in order. I am not affiliated with any manufacturer.

There are two basic pickup types, magnetic pickups and piezoelectric pickups. The latter type work with all kinds of strings (steel, nylon, or gut). Magnetic pickups work only with steel strings, and consist of magnets and coils. Single coil pickups are sensitive to magnetic fields generated by transformers, fluorescent lamps, and other sources of interference, and are prone to pick up hum and noise from these sources. Dual coil or "humbucking" pickups use two specially configured coils to minimize this interference. Because these coils are electrically out of phase, common-mode signals (i.e. signals such as hum that radiate into both coils with equal amplitude) cancel each other.

The arrangement of the magnets is different for different pickups. Some types have rod or bar magnets inserted directly in the coils, while others have magnets below the coils, and cores of soft iron in the coils. In many cases these cores are screws, so level differences between strings can be evened out by screwing the core further in or out. Some pickups have a metal cover for shielding and protection of the coils, others have a plastic cover that does not shield against electromagnetic interference, and still others have only isolating tape for protecting the wire. The magnetic field lines flow through the coil(s) and a short section of the strings. With the strings at rest, the magnetic flux through the coil(s) is constant. Pluck a string and the flux changes, which will induce an electric voltage in the coil. A vibrating string induces an alternating voltage at the frequency of vibration, where the voltage is proportional to the velocity of the strings motion (not its amplitude). Furthermore, the voltage depends on the string's thickness and magnetic permeability, the magnetic field, and the distance between the magnetic pole and the string.

There are so many pickups on the market that it is difficult to get a comprehensive overview. In addition to the pickups that come with an instrument, replacement pickups—many of them built by companies that do not build guitars—are also available. But to be precise: a pickup does not "have" a sound; it only has a "transfer characteristic". It transfers the sound content that it gets from the strings and alters it, every model in its own fashion. For instance: mount the same Gibson humbucker on a Les Paul and on a Super 400 CES: you will hear completely different sounds. And the best pickup is useless on a poorly designed guitar. The basic rule is always: garbage in—garbage out!

Unlike other transducers that have moving parts (microphones, speakers, record player pickups, etc.), magnetic pickups have no moving parts—the magnetic field lines change, but they have no mass.

The pickup as a circuit

When the strings are moving, they cut the magnetic field lines, inducing an alternating voltage in the coil. So the pickup acts like an AC generator with some attached electric components: an inductance "L", in series with a resistance "R", both in parallel to a winding capacitance "C". This is a simplification of reality, but quite useful to understand the way a pickup works.

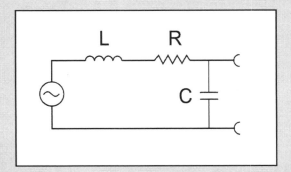

Many people measure only the resistance (measured in ohms), which is an over-simplification, and expect to know something about a pickup, which of course is a fundamental error.

By far, the most important quantity is the **inductance** (measured in Henries), which in simple terms, is a coil's capacity of generating an electrical signal via its interaction with a magnetic field. The resistance and the capacitance don't have much influence and can be neglected in a first approximation.

The external load consists of a resistance (the pots, plus any resistance to ground at the amplifier input) and a capacitance (produced between the hot lead and the shield in the guitar cable). There is also an electrical resonance between the inductance of the pickup coil and the capacitance of the guitar cable. **All this results in a resonant frequency, which exhibits an amplitude peak.** If you know those factors (the resonant frequency and height of that resonant peak), **you know about 90% of a pickup's transfer characteristics**. These two parameters are the key to the "secret" of a pickup's sound.

What all this means is:

- overtones in the range around the resonant frequency are amplified
- overtones above the resonant frequency are progressively reduced
- the fundamental vibration and the overtones far below the resonant frequency are reproduced without alteration.

(An overtone is a natural resonance of a system, in the case of a string, normally associated with the harmonics—integer multiples of the fundamental frequency). The above mentioned cable capacitance must not be neglected. Since different guitar cables have different amounts of capacitance, it is clear that using different cables will change the resonant frequency and hence the overall sound.

There are some books that deal especially with electric guitar pickups. **They pay much attention to the resistance and the magnet materials.** But the resistance is the *least* interesting magnitude of all. And statements like "Alnico 5 sounds like this, Alnico 2 sounds like that" are completely misleading. Many "pickup experts" have never heard the term "inductance". What you find in those books is an obsolete "geocentric" view on pickups that will never work.

The integral "heliocentric" view on pickups: Pickup, pots in the guitar, cable capacitance, and amp input impedance **are an interactive system that must not be split up into its parts**. If you analyze the properties of the parts separately you will never understand how the system works as a whole. The sound material a pickup receives from the strings is not flavored by the pickup alone but by the complete system.

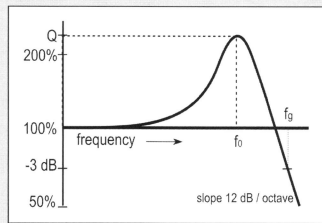

Fundamental frequency response of a magnetic pickup. Position and height of the peak vary, which constitutes the response of a particular pickup.

As said above, this includes the guitar cable. Another cable, another sound! This is a shame but it is true. You can easily check it up. A few pickup manufacturers know that fact but they conceal it. The majority seems to be totally ignorant.

How resonance affects Sound

The resonant frequency of most available pickups in combination with normal guitar cables lies between 2,000 and 5,000 Hz. This is the range where the human ear has its highest sensitivity. A quick subjective correlation of frequency to sound is that at 2,000 Hz the sound is warm and mellow, at 3,000 Hz brilliant or present, at 4,000 Hz piercing, and at 5,000 Hz or more brittle and thin. The sound also depends on the peak's height: a high peak produces a powerful, characteristic sound; a low peak produces a weaker sound. In most pickups, the peak ranges between 1 and 4 (0 to 12 dB).

Single coil vs. humbuckers response

The results presented in the figures (how resistance and capacitance affect sound) are really only precise for single coil pickups. Humbucking pickups have certain notches at high frequencies, because the vibrations of the strings are picked up at two points simultaneously. High overtones, where the peaks and the valleys of the waveform occur simultaneously in two poles, can produce cancellations. The difference on the sound between one coil and two coils with a humbucker is overestimated. The main reason for getting more treble with one coil is that the resonant frequency has been raised because of the halving of the inductance. Sensing the strings at only one point instead of two also has an effect, but this is much smaller. It can only be compared when the resonant frequency is held constant while switching.

In any case, more important than the type of pickup you are using (single coil or humbucker), is the resonance curve itself. Look at the response represented in the figure below. Is a "Hoyer" pickup, built around 1970, looking like a humbucker but with only one coil inside, with a capacitance of 470 pF, showed under five different resistive loads. With the 250 k pots used in this guitar, there is no more resonance because of very strong "eddy currents" (induced magnetic fields that oppose the change of the original magnetic field) in the metal parts. The sound is dull, and the resonance curve shows exactly that.

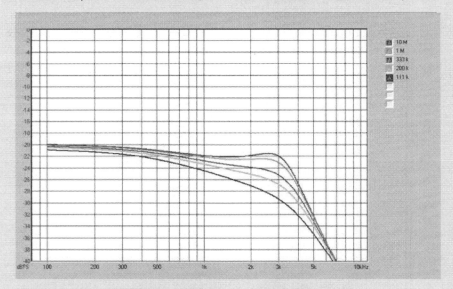

Response of an inferior quality pickup. It shows no resonant frequency peak.

Summary

I propose to adopt an integral view on sound that involves pickups, potentiometers, cable capacitance, and amplifier input impedance. The signal received from the strings is not "flavored" by the pickup alone but by the complete system. If we analyze the properties of the parts separately we will never understand how the system works as a whole.

Matching pickups

Most electric guitars made up to around the 70's (including Fenders and Gibsons) generally used the same pickups in all positions, so it was the pickup position alone that generated different sounds. These days, it is more common to combine different pickup types, and use hotter (higher output) pickups in the bridge position.

The usual configuration is to combine a super-hot, high-output bridge pickup with a clean neck pickup. Another common solution along similar lines, and even more extreme, is to use a single coil in the neck position and a humbucker in the bridge position. A great idea in theory, and fine if they are the only two sounds you want. But when you combine these pickups (in the usual way–in parallel and in phase, no active electronics) it doesn't sound very different from the *weaker* neck pickup on its own.

You might have expected the hot bridge pickup to dominate, but the opposite happens! This is caused by an impedance mismatch between the pickups, and the lower impedance single coil drains much of the sound of the higher impedance humbucking pickup. The lower impedance neck pickup, however, is hardly affected by the higher impedance bridge pickup.

Pickup "mismatches" are consequences of trying to go for too much variety on the same instrument, particularly if you play live. These are some ways to avoid such pitfalls:

- At best, combine pickups with similar output values (similar inductance). As long as the bridge pickup is the same or a little more than the neck, they will mix well. Consider the example of the Telecaster: the bridge pickup's coil has up to 9200 turns, and the neck pickup has only about 8000. But the neck pickup uses a slightly thinner wire, which balances the inductance of the two pickups, making a great matching pair.

- With a stereo setup of the pickups you can optimize the sound of each pickup. You will need a more complex treatment of the sound on the amplification part of the chain, though (stereo amp or two amps).

- Many pickup manufacturers offer neck/bridge sets of pickups, where the bridge pickup has a few extra coil turns to give it a slightly hotter output (to compensate for less string vibration over the bridge pickup) and a little more midrange tone, to evenly match the tone of the neck pickup.

- The use of active electronics can solve mismatch problems.

Solo switching

Some players simply want to switch between a low-level rhythm sound and a high level solo sound with the pickup selector switch. The two pickups are unlikely to mix together well, but if you don't use the sound of both pickups at the same time, it doesn't matter anyway. A common setup for such "solo switching" configuration is: installing a hot humbucker at the bridge, combined with a much lower inductance pickup at the neck (for example a single coil or a vintage humbucker). Remember, solo switching implies loosing the sounds derived from combining multiple pickups, though.

Matching passive and active pickups

It can be done, as long as the passive pickup has a preamp, or the active has a resistor in series so it behaves like a passive one. Of course in the latter case, there is no point in having an active pickup. Generally, this combination isn't worthwhile, unless you enjoy experimenting with electronics.

Check the websites of the principal pickup brands for suggestions on how to combine their pickups (find a list of the brands on Appendix C, at the end of the book). Some offer sound samples and interactive tools to compare other combinations. You don't necessarily have to buy those, but it might be interesting to understand the matching criteria used by the manufacturers themselves.

Pickup placement

Where do I place the pickups? In a place that allows each pickup to better fulfill its mission.

Plucked strings vibrate in a complex way, a superposition of several vibration modes activated simulta-

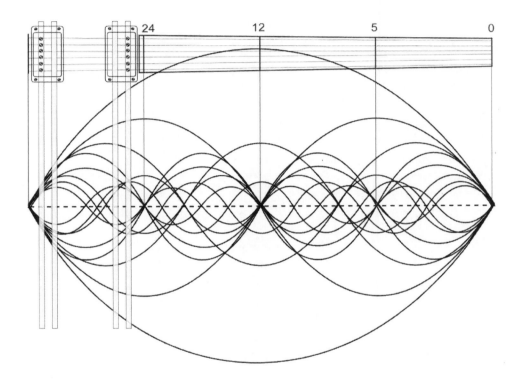

neously. In the next figure, the sinusoidal curves represent the first eight vibration modes:

The biggest curve represents the fundamental mode, and each subsequent overtone has less amplitude and higher frequency than the previous one—*ad infinitum*. **The four vertical grey bars mark the location of the pickups' magnets, and show how each pickup "reads" the different vibrations.** Changing the placement of the pickups changes the way each vibration mode is perceived by the pickup. In the example, the gray bars (i.e., the magnets) do not meet any nodes, that is, the points at which the curves values are zero.

The myth of the node at the 24th fret

It is often said that if a pickup (or more properly, its magnets) were placed under the node at the 24th fret, three of the principal eight modes would simply not be perceived by the pickup, because three overtone curves have a *zero* value at that particular point. Such a situation is not unusual on guitars (or some basses) with 20, 21, or 22 frets: the neck pickup often ends up placed under that point, one fourth the distance from the bridge. But the graphic above only shows the nodes created by the vibration of the open strings. Each fretted string gets its vibrating length shortened, so a new configuration of nodes emerges; the cancellations occur in different places for each fret!

Additionally, magnetic pickups have wide "apertures": they sense a pretty big length of the string, not the string at just *one* point (humbuckers, doubly so). So even when they are located right under a node they still read string vibration around that node, too.

That makes it impossible, from a practical standpoint, to avoid all nodes for all frets. In short, trying to avoid (or meet) any tonal node is a non-issue. Yes, the sound may vary with millimetrical pickup position changes–but there is simply no "mathematical", "correct" way to place pickups, because the resulting, slightly different sounds are not *objectively* good or bad, they are simply different.

What is the **practical** *way to place pickups, then?*

- **Bridge pickup**: in electric guitars the bridge pickup is placed a few millimeters away from the bridge. The nearer the bridge, the more "trebly" the tone will be, with lower output level (due to the shorter amplitude of the string vibration at that point). Changes in pickup placement near the bridge are far more noticeable than those near the neck position.

  In basses, it is better to place the bridge pickup not so close to the bridge: we need it where those fat strings are vibrating enough. Depending on the scale and personal preferences, the distance from pickup to bridge could be 1" (25.4 mm) or more. Check the measurements of basses of the *same scale* as yours whose sound pleases you. Placing the pickups in an analogous way will likely produce an analogous dynamic response (not necessarily a similar *tonal* response, though, unless you use the same pickups).

- **Neck pickup**: in guitars, place the pickup close to the end of the fretboard. In general, the closer to the fretboard the better, since the sound will be mellower and louder. If the truss rod adjustment is at the body end of the neck, space will have to be provided between the end of the neck and the neck pickup for the truss rod adjustment to be made.

  In basses, leave some space between the end of the fretboard and the neck pickup to provide room for slap style playing if the instrument will be used in this fashion.

Slanted pickups

Some luthiers don't place the pickup perpendicular to the strings, but at a slight angle. The magnets of the treble strings get closer to the bridge, and the magnets that "read" the bass strings become gradually more separated from the bridge. This is done to increase the *tonal range response* of the instrument, since the treble strings will sound more "twangy", more brittle, and the bass strings will sound more "bassy" (see figure):

Does it work? Yes, the response of the pickup should be audibly different.

Is it better? That depends on the sound you are looking for. Again, there is no mathematical recipe. Is all about testing different angles, and checking the results. Slanting is not recommended for humbuckers, though. The magnets will not end up in line with the strings. Slanting single coils in too big an angle will cause the same situation (see graphic on next page). Using pickups with magnetic *rods* instead of individual magnets for each string will eliminate the problem.

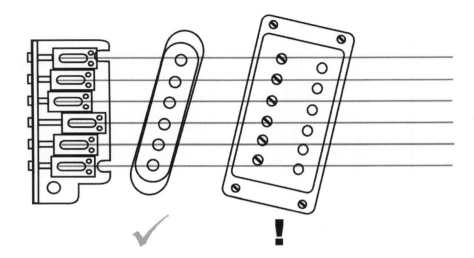

Slanting pickups might improve the response range... as long as the strings stay above the magnets!

Pickup cavities

As their name indicates, they are cavities routed in the front of the instrument, to accommodate the pickups. Pickup cavities follow standard dimensions, which in turn depend on the standard measurements of the different pickup models.

See Appendix D for templates of guitar and basses pickup cavities - those drawings don't include depth measurements for all models though, since it is better to calculate as a function of the size of the pickup to be used. The depth of the cavity will also depend on the distance between the strings and the instrument's top, since some pickup models are fastened by screwing them to the base of the cavity, and if the cavity is too deep the installation will be problematic.

Checklist

1: Choosing pickups

● **A good sound depends on a lot of factors, but the pickup quality is one under your direct control.** Go for the best you can find. Most manufacturers offer sound samples of their products; check them out online. Remember: "more expensive" doesn't necessarily mean "better quality" (although normally "cheap" implies *low quality*).

● **The real parameter shaping the quality of a pickup** is its resonance curve. Do not rely only on its resistive value.

● **Pickup style must match musical style.** Let us not forget that the ultimate product of lutherie is not the guitar, but the music. Avoid obvious incompatibilities, like installing super-hot, active, raging pickups on a jazz guitar. There are many excellent pickups which will work well for very diverse genres, though.

● **For perfectionists.** Make sure the pickup pole spacing matches the spread of the strings, even though pickups dimensions are pretty standard.

- **So, humbuckers, or single coils?** The difference between the two types is commonly described as follows: single coils are *bright and clear*, humbuckers are *warm and fat*. That is consistent with the following relations:

    Single coils have lower inductance $\longrightarrow$ lower output $\longrightarrow$ higher resonant frequency $\longrightarrow$ brighter tone (more high tones present).

    Humbuckers have higher inductance $\longrightarrow$ higher output $\longrightarrow$ lower resonant frequency $\longrightarrow$ warmer tone (more mid tones present).

2: Matching pickups

(These considerations apply to fully passive circuits only):

- **Humbuckers and single coils don't go well together,** unless they have compatible inductance (which is rare).
- **Power and clarity–choose one.** Low impedance pickups will get you the cleanest, purest tones–but lower output. High impedance pickups will produce a stronger, higher output, meaner sound. **"Hot" and "mellow" don't go well together.** Try to match pickups with a similar inductive values, or at least similar resistances. Or use active electronics (see chapter 11– "Electronics")
- **Ideally,** you will find a set of pickups that have a similar tonal balance while still allowing the natural timbre to shine through. This usually means a hotter bridge pickup with more mids and basses and a vintage neck pickup with more highs. That way, you don't have to compromise anything with your amp tone settings and you have a wide selection of different sounds.

3: Placing pickups

- In guitars, close to the bridge is good; basses need a little more distance.
- **Slanting**: okay for single coils (within reason), but in general not for humbuckers.

Additional advice:

- **For perfectionists.** Check how the pickups sound with and without a metallic cover. The metallic cover will induce currents in itself, absorbing energy and *flattening* the resonance curve a little bit. Sometimes this is perceptible, and in general, pickups will sound a little better without the cover. They look nice, though–another trade-off to resolve. Or not.

After all calculations and discussions have been pursued to exhaustion, the only important thing is the **sound**. Go to a music shop (or visit a collector friend, if you have one) and spend an afternoon trying different guitars. That will give you valuable insights, and not only about pickups!

10 CONTROL DESIGN

- **Type of controls: volume, tone, blend, etc.**
- **Master controls and individual controls**
- **Switches: types and functions**
- **"Mods": series/parallel, in/out of phase**
- **Knobs and jack plates**
- **Placement of the controls**

"I really wanted to be Jacqueline du Pré on cello. So I started playing. But you have to give your whole life to a cello. When I realized that, I went back to the guitar and turned the volume up."

—Ritchie Blackmore (British guitarist, founder of Deep Purple)

The basics

Philosophy of control design
Keep it simple

Controls affect the signal transferred by the pickups, and consequently the sound. Nothing else, nothing less.

The guitar controls are the interface between the player and the instrument. That fact can lead to the mistaken conclusion that the more controls the guitar has, the more control the player has over the instrument. But in fact, designing an instrument with too many controls can lead to these problems:

- All the cluttered knobs and switches interfere with each other, either physically (they are too close to each other) or functionally.

- The operation of the instrument gets complicated.

- You get control over more variables, but not all of them are usable or necessary. For example, by using three 3-way switches you can produce up to 21 sound variations (splitting coils, putting them in phase, out of phase, etc.), but probably only 4 or 5 of them are interesting–the same number of sounds you can obtain with a single lever switch.

- Too many controls can affect the visual "purity" of the instrument.

"Mapping"

The controls should follow good conceptual design, correctly *mapping* the instrument's operation. Les Pauls have four knobs, and I always have to start plucking strings and turning knobs to deduce what happens, because their function changes from instrument to instrument. And then I have to remember what the knobs do.

The Stratocaster's controls aren't very intuitive, either. There are 3 pickups, which are supposed to be controlled by one volume pot (so far so good, it *has* to be a master-volume, obviously) but then you have *two* tone controls. You know they are tone controls because they have the word "TONE" written on them. Two tone knobs for three pickups. How is that supposed to work? You have to check the manual...

Using spatial analogies whenever possible is the essence of good mapping controls. For example, if you have a guitar with two pickups with individual volume controls, the knob closer to the neck should control the neck pickup, and the knob closer to the bridge, the bridge pickup.

A good control should also provide information on the precise state the device is in, which doesn't normally happens with guitars. If you look at a slide control, you instantly know the level at which it is set. Sliders are not the best for guitars though, because without looking at them you don't know where in the scale the slide is at a given moment. This means you have to feel around for the knob. Circular pots on the other hand are always in the same place, but reading the current status is not so simple.

Another example: some guitars let you know if they are connected or not. A small *led* that goes on when the instrument is receiving electrical current is an interesting system status device (the Yamaha RGX series comes to mind).

Electric guitar and bass controls

The controls you can find in a conventional guitar or bass are **volume controls, tone controls** (or more generally, "equalization controls"), and **switching devices**. Let's review them in detail.

In depth

Volume control

If you are designing a guitar with only one control, it will be a volume control–the most basic control on a guitar. If the volume control affects the instrument as a whole (that is, all pickups simultaneously), then it is called a "master volume" control.

The volume control consists, of course, in affecting how intense is the signal delivered from the instrument to the amplifier (understood physically in terms of the signal's amplitude).

The design decision narrows to having a master volume, or independent volumes for each pickup. Such a decision involves *functionality vs. flexibility* tradeoff. Have you seen the controls of the legendary (and oh-so beautiful) Alembic basses? They have so many knobs that it seems like you could control the Space Shuttle's atmosphere reentry and landing from there. Totally flexible, but at some cost in complexity.

Independent volume controls for each pickup allow for more sound variants, but you have to adjust two controls alternately until you reach the desired level. In a live performance (dark stage, real time) a master volume would be more practical.

The problem with independent controls for each pickup

In the market there are many models with this dual-control configuration. Les Pauls have two controls for tone (the same as Stratocasters) and two controls for volume. The same with basses: the Fender Jazz Bass uses two volumes.

If you want to have independent controls for each pickup in your instrument, beware of a problem that arises with the electronics: turning down one volume control affects *both* pickups. This happens because the volume controls are in parallel, and when either of the controls is turned down the whole output signal is "short-circuited" to **ground** (called "earth" in the United Kingdom and Australia, among others).

The common solution is simply *reversing* the input and output connections (see wiring diagram in chapter 11). **But beware!** This creates *another* problem: as long as the controls are at maximum, the signal from the pickups is transferred without problem. But as soon as you turn any volume control down, the *peak of the resonant frequency* (discussed in the previous chapter) gets *lower*, resulting in a dull sound. With the volume at 80%, the sound would already have lost expressivity. Playing with even lower volume levels would produce a patently unimpressive sound.

The same will happen when using independent tone controls. The effect can be minimized by connecting some extra capacitors or virtually eliminated by using active electronics.

Blender control

A blend (sometimes called "balance") control is an interesting feature. It is a pot that controls the volume of 2 pickups at the same time. It has a middle position, at which both pickups are at 100% volume.

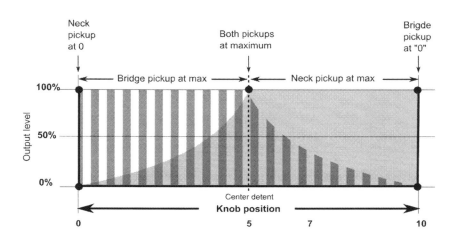

If you set the control to one of the extremes, you get 100% from one pickup, and zero volume from the other, depending on the direction in which you turned the control.

In the previous graphic, when the control is on one of the ends, only one pickup works (either the bridge or the neck pickup). When the control is at the center position (in "5"), both pickups are at maximum. Turning the knob one way or the other creates all volume combinations in between.

The problem with blender controls

A blend control combines well with a master volume control. But attention: using a blender and a master volume control without inserting a buffer amp between them results in the same kind of problem you get with other multi-pot control circuits (acting on one pot affects both pickups).

For all practical purposes a blender pot is recommended only when used in a circuit with *active* electronics (that is, with a preamplification of the signal on the instrument). Pickup selection switches (like the ones in Les Pauls and Strats) are simpler and quicker to operate, though, that's why many players prefer them instead of a blender control.

Tone control (or equalization controls)

The function of a tone control is, by means of filtering selected frequencies, to produce a more "trebly" or "bassy" signal, that is, with more or less *high* harmonics. Using independent tone controls for each pickup (or group of pickups) is a popular choice: it is the standard way Les Pauls are built. But again: the two tone controls will present the same problem we encounter with two volume controls!

Multiple tone controls are not unusual in guitars that combine single coil pickups with humbuckers, as each pickup needs to be associated with electronic components with diverse characteristics (more in next chapter).

A master tone is the most practical solution, though: both in professional and amateur contexts, more involved equalization can be done more effectively on either a console or the amplifier.

A more sophisticated version of a tone control would be to have equalization controls (EQ), composed of several knobs, which are used to affect particular ranges of frequencies. The most common implementation is a 3-way EQ configuration, to control highs, mids and low frequencies separately. This is frequently found on basses with active electronics.

No controls at all!

The pickups can be connected directly to the jack, and all parameters controlled directly from the amp. This unusual option could make some sense in a concept guitar, an artistic instrument, a minimalist bass. In practice it is *not* recommended unless you are working on an instrument with a total priority of form over functionality. Problems you can find on an instrument without controls, apart from losing influence on the instrument's response:

- The pickups will have no resistive load (there are no controls whatsoever). This will affect the sound of the instrument in ways that deserve a test before deciding to go with this option; in general, the sound will be too brittle.

- The guitar will probably be too "sensitive"; you will hear each movement of your fingers on the strings.

- If you get that horrible feedback noise through your amp, you will have to dampen the strings with your hand, or walk to the amp to lower the volume.

Switches

The formal definition of *switch* describes them as components that can break an electrical circuit by interrupting the current or diverting it from one conductor to another.

Function

Switches are used:

1. To select which pickup/s are on

2. For "coil tapping", which means to make a dual coil humbucking pickup work as if it were a single coil pickup, by switching one of the coils out of the circuit. It is a useful feature which provides single-coil sounds from a guitar equipped with humbuckers (but only if they are the "4-wire" type of humbuckers). But coil tapping will produce a drop in the output, which according to my experience is something not favored by all musicians. The resulting sound is not comparable to a real single coil, except for a few cases of humbucker pickups which are constructed differently as the common Gibson-type ones.

3. To set the way the pickups or their coils are wired, that is, for connecting pickups or coils in *series* or in *parallel*.

"In series" means *consecutively*; the end of one element (a coil or a pickup) is connected to the beginning of the next.

This sacrifices high frequencies but delivers a fuller sound with high output, which is good for distortion.

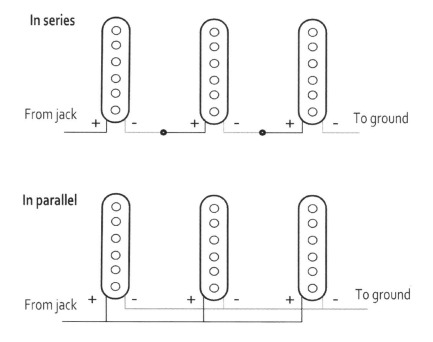

"**In parallel**" means that all the *starts* (or "inputs") of the coils are connected together, and all their ends (or "outputs") are connected together as well. This produces a brighter tone.

4. For setting coil phase relationship

Changing the phase between two pickups (or between two coils in a single pickup) means *inverting the polarity* of one of the coils. The end of a coil gets connected not to the beginning, but to the *end* of another coil (see graphic on next page). These are the possibilities:

- **Series–In phase:** is the standard way to wire the two coils of a humbucker, and the one that delivers the highest output. The lower spectrum of frequencies dominates, creating the typical warm, "smooth attack" sound of Les Pauls. As this combination is hum-canceling, there is no electromagnetic interference from lamps or other appliances.

- **Series–Out of phase:** Thinner, "funky" sound with good power.

- **Parallel–In phase:** A single coil type of sound, clear and bright due to lower output. Strong highs and good attack. Hum canceling.

- **Parallel–Out of phase:** Thinner, "funky" sound with low power.

   The out of phase options are less popular, because of the "phaser" sound, but also because they do not cancel hum. Phase effects are more noticeable if both pickups are out of phase, not just one.

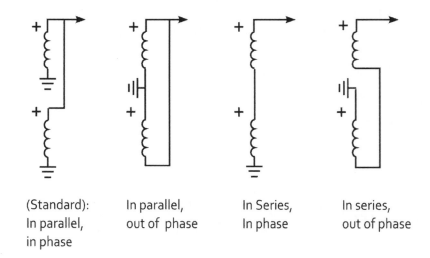

(Standard):   In parallel,   In Series,   In series,
In parallel,   out of phase   In phase   out of phase
in phase

"In phase" is the normal way to combine pickups; the "out of phase" pickups produce a thinner, more trebly sound, with less volume.

Switches used on electric guitars

The usual kind of switches used on guitars and basses are:

- **Toggle switches**
- **Lever switches**
- **Rotary switches**

Here we will review their basic characteristics. In the next chapter ("Electronics") we will go into detail regarding their construction and connection.

Toggle switches

Toggle switches have a small lever that pivots on a single point (the famous Les Paul "Rhythm/treble" switch. In the center position both pickups are on.

Lever switches

A Stratocaster has 3 pickups, so it uses a

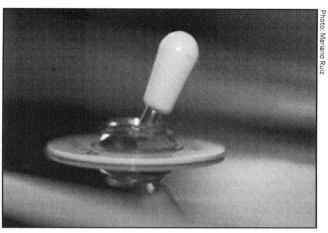

Photo: Mariano Ruiz

A three-way toggle switch, as found on Les Pauls.

5-position switch lever switch to activate the different combinations. Which pickup is activated depends on the wiring, but the standard configuration is:

1. Neck pickup only
2. Neck + middle pickups
3. Middle pickup only
4. Middle + bridge pickups
5. Only bridge pickup

...where positions "2" and "4" have a hum-canceling effect, given that the coil in the middle pickup is a *reverse-wound, reverse-polarity* pickup.

Rotary switches

A rotary switch consists of a spindle or "rotor", and a number of terminals arranged in a circle around the rotor. By turning the rotor, a different set of terminals is connected, activating the corresponding circuits. These switches have a *detent* mechanism so it "clicks" from one active position to another. In guitars, the widest known examples are some PRS guitars; each position activates a different combination of pickups/coils. A standard configuration is the following:

1–Neck pickup only
2–Coil tap (outside coils), parallel

The typical lever switch on a Stratocaster.

Rotary switch, used in this case to select among several capacitor values, affecting the resonant frequency's peak of the pickup (more info: www.gitarrenelektronik.de).

3–Coil tap (outside coils), series

4–Coil tap (inside coils), parallel

5–Bridge pickup only

Common criticism of this kind of switch when used as a pickup selector:

- It takes some time to get used to, especially for players already familiar with the 5-way lever.

- There is no position in which both humbuckers are simultaneously active. Like in a Strat, no position activates *all* pickups at the same time.

- It is harder to visually evaluate the state the pickups are in, compared to a lever switch.

Knobs

What can possibly go wrong here? It's just a plastic thingy, right? Let's see. This is a list of the possible bad or unnecessary characteristics a guitar control knob can have:

- **Wrong size.** The thinner the knob, the harder it is to control its turning. The minimal comfortable diameter for a guitar knob would be between 5/8" and 7/8" (16 to 22 mm). You need something easy enough to locate using your hands only, and thick enough to allow good and comfortable operation. But not too thick: the player must be able to move it by just wrapping the small finger around it (the rest of the hand is busy playing!).

- **Slippery surfaces** like polished ones. Much better is a knob easy to grab and operate—unless aesthetic considerations take priority. Metal knobs have normally a textured surface (called "knurling") to facilitate their operation. Plastic knobs often use ribbing to the same effect.

- **Lack of status information.** Sometimes you need to take a quick look at the knobs to know the current setting. A point, mark, graduation, metallic indicator, or some other visual reference is necessary to avoid guesswork when adjusting the controls—unless you like to play always at "11"!

- **Non-cylindrical, irregular knobs,** the kind that present edges to your fingers instead of surfaces. For example, "chicken head" knobs (designed for amplifiers front panels, not guitars), dice-shaped knobs, skull-shaped knobs, etc. They can (sometimes) be cool, but they aren't ergonomic.

Jack plate

The location of the jack plate is typically on the side (Les Paul) or on the top of the instrument (Strat). There is not much need to innovate here: you want to keep the plug as far away from your body as possible. Telecasters have a good jack plate: discreet, sober, and in the form of a "mini-funnel", which makes it easy to insert the plug. The Jack plate of the Strat is somewhat like that, too, and it is on the top of the instrument, which further simplifies the insertion of the cable plug, because you can see what you are doing. And they look nice. Using them in a guitar of our own design would be practical, but not original at all, though; it's one of those things that just scream "Fender".

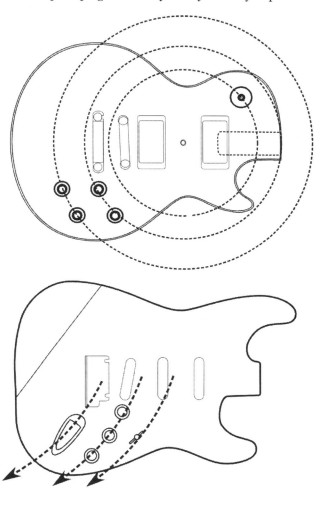

Control placement

Where should the controls be placed? Once again, let's use the classics as case studies.

In a Les Paul, the controls are disposed in a rhomboidal fashion, but they can be perceived as located on concentric circles centered on the exact middle point of the guitar's waist. Notice also how the two volume knobs lay on a curve that inscribes the upper bout, creating a harmonious distribution of the elements.

On a Strat, the controls are located on a line that follows the natural movement of the playing hand: the arc that a playing hand would follow when the player's forearm pivots at the elbow. The first knob is easy to find without having to look at it. Note how the rest of the elements (jack, switch) follow coherent lines, too. That is human-based design!

In any case, do not place the controls too close to the strings; it would interfere with the playing–i.e. you could hit them when doing a chord's follow-through. But do not place them too far away, either: the playing hand needs to be able to quickly go from strings to controls, and back; some playing techniques even require operating the controls *while* playing (example: "Cathedral", by Van Halen–look it up on YouTube).

Checklist

Well designed controls

Paul Stanley said: *"A good guitar only needs a volume knob and a tone knob. If you can't make it with that, then you need a new guitar"*. So, well designed controls should be:

- **Intuitive.** It must be easy to understand, by their physical distribution alone, which pots or switches control which variables.

- **Flexible** enough, but not redundant.

- **Practical**, oriented to the basic functions of the instrument.

- **Easy and comfortable to operate** (think knob shape, size, and spacing).

- **Distributed in a way that makes sense with the geometry of the body shape, or with ergonomics**–or with both.

- **Distributed in a way that prioritize access to master controls over individual controls.** The most used control (generally a master volume) should be placed close to the bridge.

- **Ideally, all sound settings should be attainable with no more than two actions.** If you have to touch more than two switches or pots to change from one configuration to another, you might need to reevaluate your choice of controls.

Additional advice:

- **Avoid designing an instrument without controls.** Want to build an experimental guitar? Even if the "looks" have a total priority, try to conceal the controls somehow, but do not sacrifice them, if possible.

- **Toggle or lever switches?** Each one has its advantages. Lever switches allow more positions, but are more difficult to install; the shaft of the lever needs a slot routed on the pickguard or the guitar top (made with an extra-small router bit, not without difficulty). Toggle switches only need a hole of the right size–but you get three positions instead of five (enough for two pickups, though).

Once you have decided which controls your new instrument will have, all that you need to do is implement that interface on the physical plane. We need to get into guitar *electronics*.

Why is that pot covered with tape? Because that is the "smoke shooting" control, and we don't want anyone turning it on by accident!

GUITAR AND BASS
ELECTRONICS

- **Pots and caps: types, values and influence on sound**
- **Classic wiring diagrams**
- **Ground connection: avoiding noise and shocks**
- **Active and passive electronics: pros and cons**
- **How to connect the electronic components**

[NIGEL TUFNEL]:	(with strong British accent and chewing gum) *You see, most blokes, you know, will be playing at "ten". You're on "ten" on your guitar. Where can you go from there? Where?*
[MARTY DiBERGI]:	*I don't know.*
[NIGEL TUFNEL]:	*Nowhere. Exactly. What we do is, if we need that extra push over the cliff, you know what we do?*
[MARTY DiBERGI]:	*Put it up to eleven.*
[NIGEL TUFNEL]:	*Eleven. Exactly. One louder.*
[MARTY DiBERGI]:	*Why don't you just make "ten" louder, and make "ten" be the top number, and make* that *a little louder?*
[NIGEL TUFNEL]:	(After a pause, somewhat confused): *These go to* eleven.

–from "This is Spinal Tap", directed by Rob Reiner, USA, 1984.

The basics

The objective of this chapter is to help you draw the wiring diagram of your new guitar.

The control variables we discussed in the last chapter from an *interface* standpoint will now be considered as physical components. All controls will have a physical counterpart, in the form of an electronic component (or more than one), and the wiring diagram is where the controls' *design* becomes *specification*.

Electronic components

Potentiometers

Pots are the physical counterpart of volume and tone controls. They are *variable resistors*.

With a volume pot you regulate how much of the signal delivered by the pickups will reach the amplifier. A guitar at full volume has a pot which is not interfering with the signal; a guitar at *zero volume,* on the contrary, has its volume pot routing the whole signal to *ground*.

A *tone* pot works similarly, but connected in a way that only affects some of the signal's *frequencies*, not the signal as a whole, regulating which of them (and in which amount) are allowed to reach the amp.

Pots are classified according to two main parameters:

- The *taper,* which can be *linear* or *logarithmic*.
- The value, measured in *kilo ohms*— symbol: KΩ, or simply "K".

A potentiometer. Note the split, knurled shaft, so different kind of knobs can be fitted to it.

Pot taper

A "linear" pot **translates the turning of its shaft to a uniform variation** of the signal; a logarithmic pot follows a curve like the one in the figure. Pots used in electric guitars are usually **logarithmic,** because the human ear's perception of loudness is also logarithmic (sound intensity is measured in deci-

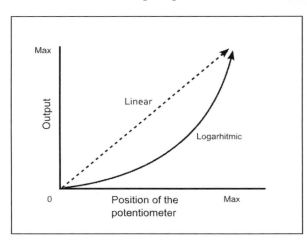

bels, which is correlated logarithmically with the sound energy, measured in Joules). Using a linear pot, it would seem as if the volume "jumps" too suddenly, as if all the change were too abrupt at the middle of the scale, instead of gradual. Logarithmic pots (also called "audio taper pots") provide a much smoother control of the volume. Of course, you can use a linear pot for volume, if that suits your personal taste. But not major USA manufacturer uses linear pots and no major USA guitar parts supplier stocks linear pots. **For *tone* controls we use logarithmic pots only,** for an analogous reason.

Pot value

The most common values for volume pots are **250K** for single coil pickups and **500K** for humbuckers.

The lower the value of the pot, the more the high frequencies *bleed* to ground, and high frequencies need to be preserved more on humbuckers than on single coils, otherwise the sound could be too "warm".

Pots with a value of 1 mega-ohm (1000K, or **1M**) are the brightest sounding, and sometimes deliver best results when used with high output pickups. On standard pickups, a 1M pot might sound too brittle.

For active guitars (whose circuits include preamplifiers) **25K** is the standard value of both volume and tone pots, a pretty low resistance compared to those used in passive circuits.

However, none of the above is written in stone, and the best guide is the sound itself. Try for yourself and decide which one you like the most.

"Push/pull" and "push/push" pots

Push/pull pots are interesting components; they consist of a pot and a switch. By including both roles in one component, adding functionality without adding more knobs. They are used:

- To control a pickup's volume **and** tone
- To control volume **or** tone, **and** a "mod" (coil tapping, series/parallel, or phase mod).

Push/push work similarly, but they have a spring-loaded shaft, so the switching between its two possible states is always made by always *pushing* the knob, simplifying the operation.

Dual concentric controls

Do you remember those old car radios with two concentric knobs? The outer knob was for finding the stations, and the central knob ws for the volume. That was a dual potentiometer. Using them, a Les Paul could be controlled using 2 dual knobs instead of the usual 4, for example.

But then a little paradox arises. Dual knobs *simplify* the controls, but not the operation, because they don't *map* the instrument's variables as well as 4 single knobs. Controlling two variables from one place needs time to get used to. Dual controls are mostly seen on basses with active circuits and equalization, to reduce the total number of knobs.

How potentiometers affect sound [26]

The impact of the pots on the sound can be dramatic, and some experimentation will no doubt be worthwhile. They affect the sound (the resonance peak) depending on their quantity, their value, and how are they connected to each other:

- More pots in a circuit (and the higher their value) = higher resistance of the circuit = more highs are transferred to the amp.
- If resistors are wired in series (end to end) their values *add*. A 500K pot in series with another 500K resistor is the same as one 1000K (1M) resistor. But in virtually all guitar control wiring, pots are added in parallel, and then their values *divide*. Two 500K pots are equivalent to a resistance of only 250K.

---

[26] *Helmuth Lemme,* „"Elektrogitarren - Sound und Technik".

The following graphic shows the frequency response of a 1972 Fender Stratocaster Pickup with constant capacitive load (470 pF) and **eight different resistances** (pots are resistors, remember) from 10K to 10M.

It can be seen how different values of pots in the guitar influence the height of the resonance peak. With 47K or less the peak vanishes.

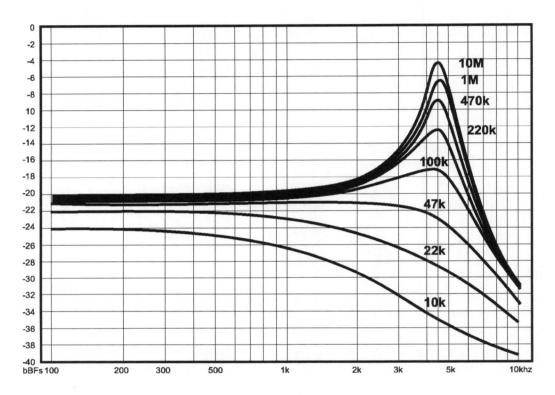

Different potentiometers (or the total number and values of them) strongly influences the sound.

Capacitors

Use of capacitors for tone control

A tone control is created by wiring a capacitor to a tone pot, creating an "adjustable filter". This means when the tone pot is turned, only the low frequencies pass to the output jack and the high frequencies are grounded out (cut).

The capacitor value determines the "cutoff frequency" of the filter (the frequency below which no high harmonics are lost), and the position of the tone pot determines how strong the reduction will be.

Keep in mind that the capacitor value only affects the sound when the tone control is being used (pot in the bass setting–knob turned towards the position "10", or *maximum*). The tone capacitor value will have little to no effect on the sound when the tone pot is in the treble setting (knob turned towards "0").

Cap values

Standard values of capacitors used in electric guitars and basses are, in ascending order, 0.001, 0.01, 0.022, 0.047 and 0.1 µf ("microfarads"–abbreviated "µf" or "MFD".).

The following chart shows their typical values, the instruments in which we commonly find them, and how they affect the passing of the different ranges of frequencies (the darker zones are the frequencies blocked by the different capacitors). Larger capacitors will have lower cutoff frequency and sound darker in the bass setting because a wider range of frequencies is being reduced. Smaller capacitors will have a higher cutoff frequency and sound brighter in the bass setting because only the ultra high frequencies are cut. For this reason, dark sounding guitars like Les Pauls with humbuckers typically use .022 MFD capacitors to cut off less of the highs and guitars like Strats and Teles with single coils typically use .047 MFD capacitors to allow more treble to be rolled off.

The key to finding the right capacitor doesn't come from a graphic though–it comes from trying different alternatives. Capacitors affect the sound signature of the pickup, so investing some time on such tests will certainly pay dividends in terms of good sound.

How capacitors affect the resonant frequency [28]

Other than using a tone pot to change the tone of a guitar (that is, connecting a capacitor in parallel with the pickup), another way to change the sound is to replace the standard tone control potentiometer with a rotary switch ("C-Switch") that connects different capacitors across the pickup. This will give you much more sound variation than a standard tone control, with a device that is commercially available, ready to install and use.

The following graphic shows the frequency response of the same pickup, now with constant resistive load and eight different load capacitors from 47 pF to 2200 pF. The resonance frequency and so the tonal characteristics can be easily changed by varying the load capacitance. Standard tone controls just *lower* the resonant frequency by connecting a capacitor in paral-

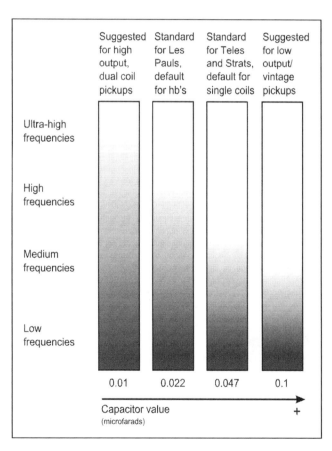

[28] *Helmuth Lemme,* „"Elektrogitarren - Sound und Technik", reproduced by his courtesy.

lel with the pickup, which also affects sound quality. A rotary switch connecting different capacitors, instead, will provide *real* sound variations by creating different resonant frequencies:

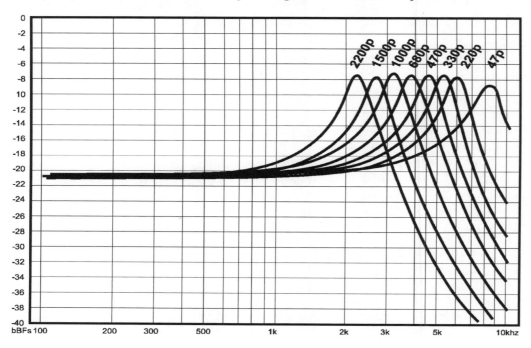

Use of capacitors for "treble bleed"

A "treble bleed" capacitor is used on a **volume** control pot to prevent treble frequency loss as the volume pot is turned down. This is done by placing a small capacitor (usually .001 MFD) between the input and output terminals of the volume control pot.

As the volume is reduced, the capacitor allows high frequencies to bleed through to the output and keeps the tone from getting muddy at lower volume settings.

In depth

Wiring examples

It would be impractical (if not impossible) to present all possible wirings in one book: for that we have the Internet. We will certainly review some popular options, but you don't necessarily need to choose among them: **you just have to find the wiring diagram that reflects the decisions you made regarding the controls you want to have.**

For this, your level of expertise is important:

If you have enough knowledge or expertise in electronics, you just design the controls you want and use that as specification, translating it into the necessary electronics.

If you are a beginner with little or no experience on electronics, these are the most practical options:

- Stick to the classic wiring diagrams shown below.
- Look for the specific circuit you want on the web sources cited in this chapter.
- Get expert help; your local guitar repairman can wire the electronics you need, or draw the diagram for you.
- Buy the electronics (either active or passive) ready to install.

For the moment let's review the different components, their functions and the way they are wired in an electronic circuit.

The block diagram

In its simplest form, a guitar's electronic circuit can be represented as follows.

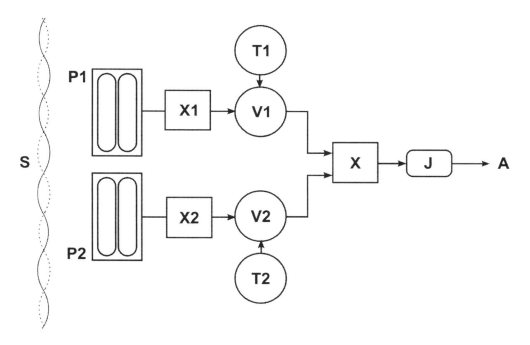

1. The **strings vibration (S)** is converted into an electrical current (the *signal*) at the **pickups (P1, P2).**

2. **A first instance of switching** occurs in X1 and X2. Here is where coil splitting, coil relationship (in/out of phase), and coil connection (series/parallel) is done.

   These can be implemented using conventional switches, or through a switching capability integrated to a potentiometer–for example in the form of push/pull pots, presented below.

3. Each signal is modified by its corresponding **volume** and **tone controls (V's, and T's).**

4. The second instance of **switching happens at X,** in this case for pickup selection.

5. **All comes together at the jack (J),** from which the signal is delivered through the cable to the **amplifier (A).**

Note that the **pickups** are always at the beginning (closer to the strings, which are the fundamental source of the sound), the **switches and pots** (which vary in number from instrument to instrument, or might even not be present at all) are in the middle, and the **jack** is always at the end. They represent the *generation, control* and *output* of the signal of an electric guitar or bass understood as a system.

Connecting components

How to connect a volume pot

In pictorial wiring diagrams **pots are always represented as seen from the bottom**, which is the position they will be in during the soldering process. They have 3 terminals (also called "lugs"): **the input** (which receives the signal from the pickup/s); **the output** (the signal, after circulating through the variable resistance, exits from the pot through this contact), and the **ground** lug.

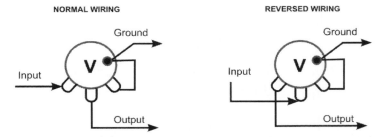

Remember the problem caused by independent volume pots? If they are wired the normal way, *both* pots will affect *both* pickups. The "solution" we presented was as to reverse the wiring, shown above.

How to wire tone pots

There are two preferred ways to attach a tone control, showed in the following figure (the standard way, and the "Les Paul" way, on the right):

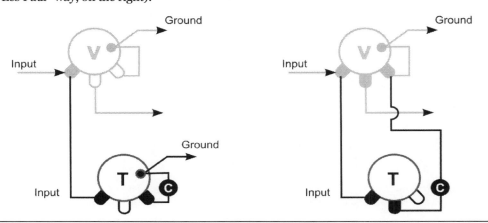

How to wire dual concentric pots

This figure shows how a dual pot is wired so you control a pickup's volume and tone from it.

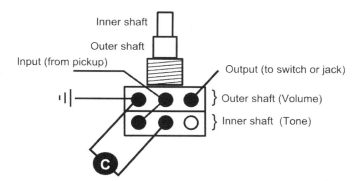

How to wire push/pull pots

These are pictorial diagrams of a push/pull pot; depending on the position of the knob (pushed or pulled), a different set of lugs of the "switch" part is on (marked in black on each figure below, and showing their internal connection). This component acts both as a pot and as a switch. Note the three lugs at the bottom: they are the potentiometer's terminals.

The particular way in which these components are wired varies with each circuit–refer to the wiring diagrams below to see some examples.

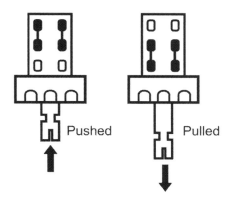

How to wire switches for pickup selection: 3-way toggle switch

A three way toggle switch is used for pickup selection in two-pickup instruments. In each of the extreme positions the small lever physically opens a contact, making the signal go through the other one. Each outer lug is connected to one of the pickups, and only in the central position can the current flow from both pickups to the jack. Refer to the Les Paul wiring diagram below for a clear view of that connection.

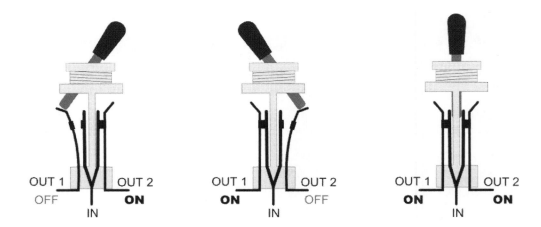

How to wire a 5-way lever switch

A 5-way lever switch consists of one common contact connected to different combinations of the other contacts by moving the lever. The figure below shows how a 5-way lever switch is wired in a Stratocaster. The precise connections vary with the particularities of each guitar, depending on the number of pick-ups, number and type of controls and function of the switch (either pickup selection, or mod setting–series/parallel, in/out of phase), etc.

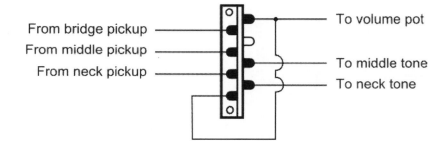

How to wire a jack

There are two types of "jack" (or "socket"): monophonic and stereo.

- **A "mono" jack** is the kind we find normally in guitars, with a "tip" lug and a "ground" lug. The "hot" wire (the one carrying the signal coming from the pickups) is soldered to the "tip" lug. A ground wire, normally coming from the back of the volume pot where all ground wires converge, is soldered (you guessed it) to the jack's "ground" lug.

- **A stereo jack** has *two* "tip" lugs, plus the "ground" lug. The signal coming from two pickups can be transported separately through a stereo cable into a stereo amplifier, or two separated amps, for example. This is not usual, though. Stereo jacks are more commonly used to turn the battery inside a guitar with active electronics on and off. That is why instruments with active circuits have to be unplugged when not in use: to avoid exhausting the battery.

Ground connection

Like in all electronic devices, electrical current circulates from a point of *higher electrical potential* (the place where the electrons are caused to start moving through the conductor) to a point of *lesser potential*. Ground is theoretically a point of zero potential, so the current will flow naturally to it. [29]

All ground wires coming from the different components in the circuit must come together at one common point. This is commonly made by soldering all grounds to the *can* of the volume pot (or one of them), and from there connected to the ground lug on the jack.

The reason to connect all ground wires to a single point (also called a "star" connection), is to avoid the so called *ground loops*. A ground loop is the result of small differences in resistance in the various signal paths to ground, which causes spurious currents through the cables, creating an audible hum.

Shielding

Shielding (called "screening" in British English) is the process of covering the instrument's cavities with a metallic medium in order to block electromagnetic interference from external sources.

Above all, it is fundamental to properly shield both the control cavity and the pickup cavities. The electronic components inside are like an antenna for all kinds of interference—motors, fridges, TVs, computers, and especially fluorescent lamps.

The materials commonly used to shield a cavity are:

- **Copper tape.** Sold in the form of leaves or rolls, it is also available with a *conductive* adhesive, and so overlapping seams are electrically continuous.
- **Conductive shielding paint.** Applied like normal paint, metallic particles suspended in this paint decant on the surface, as soon as the solvents evaporate. This is easier to apply than copper tape, especially in hard-to-reach areas.

The shielding *has* to be grounded; otherwise it will act as an antenna, worsening the hum!

If the pickups are mounted on the pickguard it is necessary to **shield the back of the pickguard** and to connect that shielding to ground, too. The most practical way of doing this is by contact: the shielding of the control cavity extends outside the cavity, over the guitar's top a little, so it makes contact with the pickguard once it is screwed into place (see photo). Control cavity covers should also be shielded in this manner.

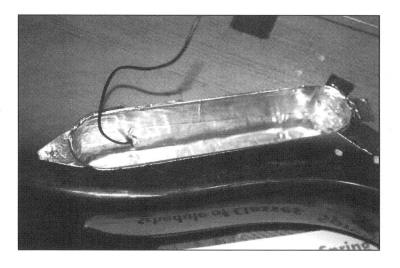

---

[29] *Think of a lightning rod, which is basically a piece of cable with one deep-interred end: irresistible temptation for lightning, which is nothing else than a massive electrical discharge!*

Grounding of the bridge

In many instruments the bridge is also connected to ground. A wire is run from the back of the volume pot to a point just under the bridge. This wire contacts the bridge when the bridge is screwed into place.

The advantage of grounding the bridge is that it reduces noise. The strings act as an antenna, picking up hum, but that source of noise is eliminated by grounding the bridge. The disadvantage is that if you touch a "live" metallic object (e.g., a faulty microphone or amp) when touching the strings, it can electrocute you.

How to avoid such a risk? These are some alternatives.

- **Ground the bridge, but install a fuse** in the ground conductor, just before it reaches the jack. Any un- wanted electrical discharge will blow the fuse, leaving the guitar without ground connection (so it may hum a little), but your life will be spared. Attention: not any fuse will do the trick. It has to be a "quick blow" fuse, of a very small value. Taylor uses this feature on their electric guitars, and the value reported for the fuse is 5 milliamperes.

- **Use low impedance circuits (active electronics and active pickups)**, which don't need bridge grounding.

- **Ground the bridge, but go wireless!** Wireless guitar systems start at around $100.

- **Consider not grounding the bridge** so the strings are totally isolated from the controls, and make sure all cavities are perfectly shielded. Connect the shielding to ground.

If you cannot stand hum, use humbuckers. If you like single coils, accept the hum as part of their charm and personality.

Additional advice to avoid electrical shock

This is not related to guitar design, but it is important advice:

- Avoid metallic pickguards on guitars with pickups mounted on them. The metallic pickguard must be connected to ground in order to effectively shield everything below it, thus becoming a risk. Use plastic pickguards, shielded only on the back.

- Avoid metallic control knobs (same issue as above), unless the pots have plastic shafts.

- Avoid older amps with 2-prong plugs. Use only electrical equipment with a dedicated, non-current carrying ground connector.

- Avoid using equipment connected to electrical outlets with two prong sockets. They are not un-common in old buildings.

Wiring diagrams: examples

Since the different possibilities are enormous, let's review the most common circuits. These diagrams show how some of the classics are wired. (Note that overlapping wires on the following figures are **not** supposed to be soldered together, unless the intersection is marked with a black dot).

On www.guitarelectronics.com *you will find more than 150 diagrams for 1, 2 or 3 pickups, series/parallel and phase switching–virtually every way there is to wire a guitar or bass.*

Precision Bass wiring

Perhaps the simplest wiring found on a classic model, the Fender Precision Bass features a single pickup with one volume and one tone control.

This instrument has a pickup that is split into two segments—each segment sensing two strings. Leo Fender's clever idea was to wire and connect these two coils in a humbucking configuration.

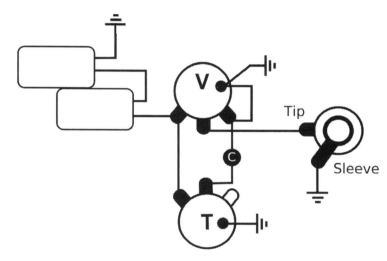

One of the simplest options for a guitar

This circuit is about the simplest electronics you can put in a guitar: one humbucking pickup with volume and tone control. The rest of the diagrams are elaborations on this one, adding more pickups and switches. Notice the ground connections on every component. Remember that those wires must be connected together, usually soldered to the can of the volume pot. From there, the ground of the volume pot itself is soldered to the sleeve of the jack.

This diagram shows a humbucker **with four wires**: they are the start and finish of both coils. There is a fifth wire: the ground (marked as "bare").

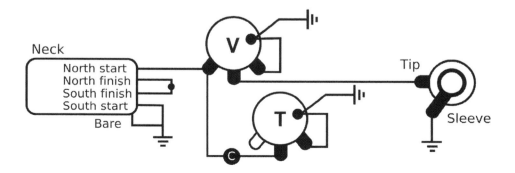

Stratocaster wiring

Three single coil pickups, master volume, 2 tone controls. Notice the similarity with the basic block diagram—except that pickup selection is done before the signal reaches the pots.

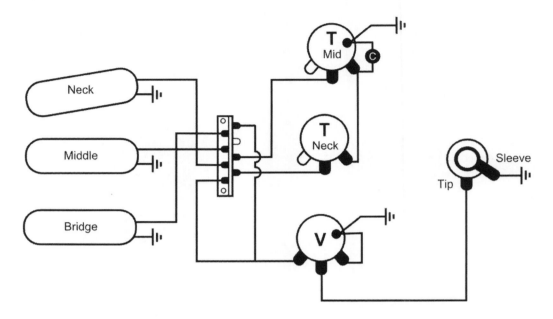

Gibson's wiring (Les Paul, SG, 335, etc.)

This is the 2-volume, 2-tone classic circuit found on Les Pauls.

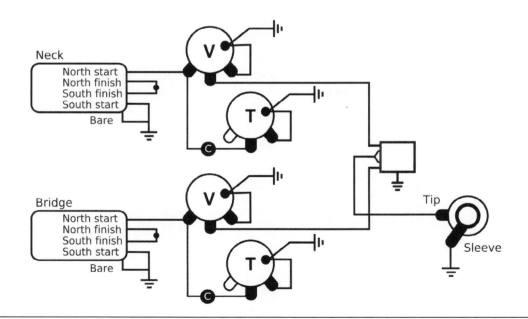

Gibsons with 3 pickups

The following circuit is used on many Gibson guitars with 3 humbuckers. Note that all pots (volume and tone) use *reverse* wiring.

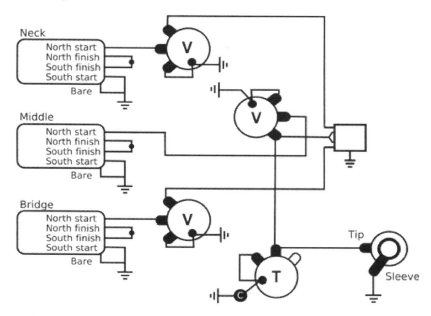

Jazz Bass wiring

The Fender Jazz Bass has a simple wiring diagram: independent volume controls (with reverse pot wiring) and a master tone control. Note that the capacitor is not wired between two pots, but directly from the middle lug to ground on the can of the tone pot.

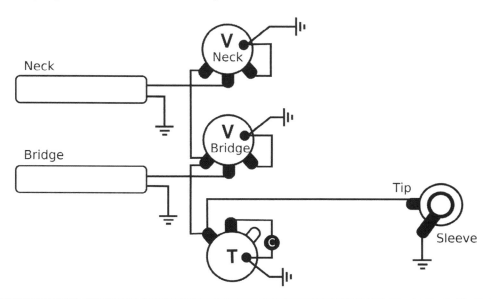

PRS wiring with rotary switch

In this diagram we see the typical PRS wiring with a rotary switch. Note that the diagram of the switch separates the two layers of contacts to make it easier to see.

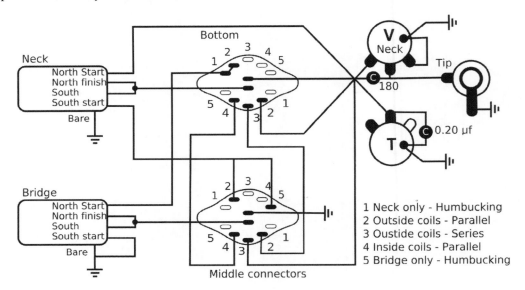

1 Neck only - Humbucking
2 Outside coils - Parallel
3 Oustide coils - Series
4 Inside coils - Parallel
5 Bridge only - Humbucking

The "Jimmy Page" Les Paul: when all possibilities collide

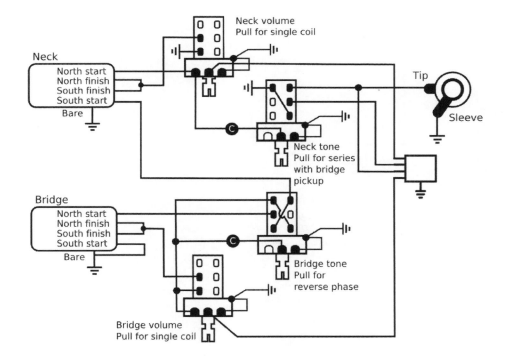

The previous figure is an example of complex wiring. In there we can find coil tapping, reverse phase, series/parallel, independent volume and tone controls, Push/pull pots, switches...

With a lot of variables under control, the last circuit represents **Jimmy Page's** preferences; if the player wants to have all these possibilities the luthier has to consider them as the primary specification to be followed, even though this might not precisely be an example of intuitive controls.

Active electronics

All wiring diagrams discussed above have *passive* components; they take the signal as provided by the pickups, eventually transform it by *taking something out of it* (intensity, frequencies, harmonics, etc), and passing it to the amplifier. Active circuits, on the other hand, introduce *pre-amplifiers*, small circuits that boost the signal from the pickups (which increases volume). That means that in this case the signal is also transformed by *adding something to it*, i.e. amplitude, or power. In fact, the main component of the circuit is one or more transistors, the solid state equivalent of a tube (the amplifying component of tube amps). The physical form of an active circuit can vary: it can consist of, for example, just an active volume pot, which is a potentiometer with the necessary electronics built-in. The active electronics can also be implemented on a small electronic board, to which the rest of the components (battery, pots, etc) are connected. Some others include equalization controls, commonly used in "active" basses.

Active circuits need an energy source to operate, normally a regular 9V battery, or two. All these components (board, battery, equalizer, pots, etc) have to be accommodated in the control cavity; the need for such additional space must be taken into account when designing the shape and size of the cavity. The pickups themselves can be *active*, too: these include the necessary circuitry to deliver an *already boosted* signal to the rest of the instrument's electronics.

Active circuit pros and cons

Pros	Cons
• Less hum than on passive circuits.	• The cost of the circuitry and pickups.
• They provide equalization capabilities on the guitar itself (when normally you have them only on the amplifier).	• The cost of the batteries.
	• No batteries, no sound–unless you switch to passive mode.
• They can provide a very clear, "hi-fi" sound or a deliciously distorted one, depending on how boosted the signal is when it reaches the amp. Passive pickups, on the other hand, sound more "crude", more "authentic".	
• More flexible and powerful controls than with passive electronics, for example for creating new sounds. They produce a strong, noise free signal, desirable for musicians who use several effects at the same time.	

You get the best of both worlds when you can switch between active and passive modes—normally using a push/pull pot to switch between them. In this case, make sure that the pickups you choose are adapted to work in both modes. Active pickups typically have fewer coil windings, giving low output, low impedance, and a very clean and clear, uncolored sound. The low output is boosted by an on-board active preamp while maintaining the low impedance. They cannot be used in passive mode.

Losing a battery in the middle of a gig is a situation that needs to be quickly solved. Instead of placing the battery in the control cavity, use a battery compartment: the battery can be replaced within seconds.

Active circuits are *not* to be considered better or worse than passive ones. They are just better adapted to certain situations or personal preferences.

Control cavity

The control cavity has the job of accommodating the guitar's electronic components.

In Les Pauls for example, the control cavity is routed in the back of the instrument, which is why they are sometimes called "*rear* control cavities". Les Pauls have also a small, circular cavity for the selector switch, located in the upper bout. The electronics remain hidden under a cover (generally made of plastic). In Stratocasters, the control cavity is routed on the front of the body. The electronics, which are mounted on the pickguard itself, remain hidden when the pickguard is set into place. Control cavity dimensions are not necessarily standard, since they may adopt several shapes and sizes depending on the room necessary to accommodate the electronics. However, rear cavity covers are sold in standard shapes and sizes. Using them will simplify things on routing day: the main guitar parts suppliers offer the corresponding routing templates.

Rear controls cavity cover

For guitars with a controls cavity on the back, two routing operations are necessary:

- First, the cavity itself, deep enough to accommodate the electronics
- Second, the recess shape for *flush mounting* the cover plate. It is only ⅛" (3 to 4 mm deep), depending on the thickness of the rear cover, but it is at least ½"wider than the cavity itself, so the screws that keep it in place can be set later on.

(Photo: Brandon McDougall from liquidguitars.com)

Rear controls cavity, just routed on the back of a Les Paul body. Notice the recess for the cover and the holes for the screws.

Control cavity depth

The cavity can be as deep as the thickness of the body allows. A 1" (25.4 mm) deep control cavity should be enough for most components (normal pots, cables, etc), but for some other components (tall push/pull potentiometers for example), the cavity must be no less than 1¼" (32 mm) deep.

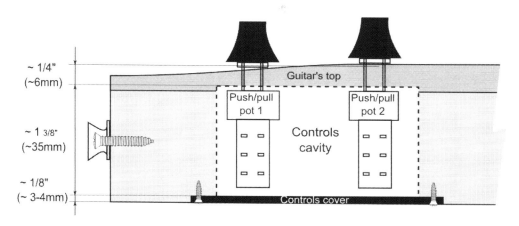

A Les Paul control cavity is 1⅞" deep, including ⅛" for the recess of the control cavity cover (48mm = 45 mm+ 3 mm for the back cover). Add the thickness of the guitar's top, and you need a body 2" thick (Les Pauls are 2 ¹³⁄₃₂"–61 mm at their thickest point).

It is also important to know the thickness the guitar top will have in the cavity's area: the top should be thick enough to be sturdy, but thin enough for the threaded collar of the potentiometers. Standard pots used for flat tops have a ⅜" tall threaded collar, which can be mounted on a pickguard, but Les Pauls and other arched top instruments use longer shaft pots, with ¾" threaded collars.

An important thing regarding the control cavity: **Internal cavities must never intersect** any bevels, cutaways, borders or recesses, or you will end up with a body with a hole in it!

Connecting cavities with "channels" for the wires

All cavities will have to be connected to each other through *internal channels,* necessary for the wires that connect all the electronic components. These are the alternatives (the arrows show from where you have to drill the hole–you will need an extra-long drill bit):

● **In Stratocasters and other models with the components mounted on the pick-guard**, you will need to drill a hole connecting the jack cavity and the control cavity.

● **In Les Pauls, or guitars with the components mounted from the inside of a rear controls cavity**, the channels must be drilled in such a way that the access point is invisible once the guitar is assembled (in the example in the photo, the hole connecting the two pickup pockets is drilled starting in the neck pocket).

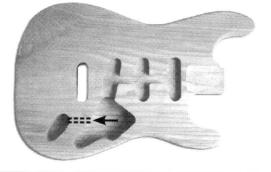

- **In guitar with bodies made of more than one piece of wood,** it is possible to route the channels on the different parts (top, body itself, back) before they get assembled. This requires careful design and preciseness during the execution (in the picture on the low right, example shown on one of my guitars. Note that I haven't used a standard rear control cavity **cover**, but a big, wooden cover–not shown on the picture).

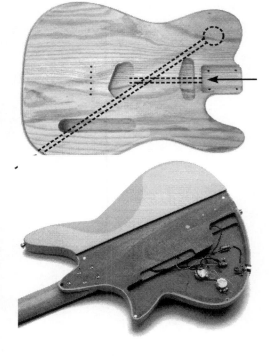

Intersecting cavities

I have built a couple of basses in which the **control cavity** intersected the **pickups cavities** inside the body, which eliminated the need to drill a channel for the wires between those cavities. The wires simply go from one cavity to the other through the resulting "common room" (marked with a circle in the figure below).

But at the end this resulted impractical, as it made it difficult to screw some pickups in place. As can be seen in the figure (a transversal section of a solid body) one of the screws has no wood underneath to be screwed to.

This wouldn't be a problem in the case of pickups mounted on rings, but it will happen with pickups that are screwed to the bottom of the pickup cavity (example: P-90 style guitar pickups and many models of bass pickups).

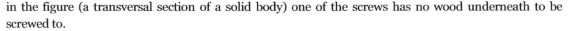

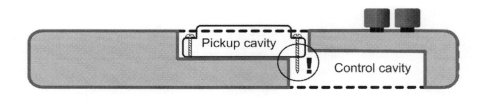

Checklist

Choosing the electronic components

- **Potentiometers for volume**: use log pots, with value 500k in humbuckers, 250K to control single coil pickups, 1M on very "hot" humbuckers (unless you enjoy trying different alternatives, which is always recommended). Active circuits usually include low value pots (25K) already.

- **Potentiometers for Tone**: use 250k pots in all tone controls. Use logarithmic pots only.

- **Capacitors**. Buy some caps of a few different values (they are really cheap), and try them to see which one suits better the sound you are looking for.

- **Remember: independent controls for each pickup will affect sound,** because it affects the resistance of the whole circuit. Use master controls and a switch to select between pickups, instead. **If you *have* to have independent controls,** then use reverse wiring and capacitors to minimize the problem. Unless you always play at maximum; but then, what's the point of having independent volume controls?

- **Push/pull pots** are a clever way to add functionality while keeping the controls simple. You can affect 2 variables at the same time, for example *volume* and *phase mod*. An out-of-phase pickup losses a little volume, which you can compensate for while your hand is on the volume control.

- **Regarding "push/pull" pots:** design the wiring in such a way that the default setting (the sound setting in which you are going to play the more) is set when push/pull pots are pushed down; that way the guitar looks "normal" most of the time. By pulling the pots up, you can switch to less used variants. Pushing the pots down again (which is easier than pulling them) allows for a quick return to the default configuration. Or just use "push/push" pots!

- **Solder all ground wires to the back of a volume pot.** It will reduce hum and noise.

- **Check the pickup color code** when using four wire humbuckers.

- **Finding the wiring diagram for your guitar:** if you happen to enjoy the design of electronic circuits, go ahead and figure out by yourself what is the physical counterpart of your controls. Otherwise, don't bake your noodle trying: all variables have been documented–just check the web resources given in this chapter and you will find what you are looking for or at least something very similar, easy to customize. A friend with some experience or your local repair shop can help, too

(Photo courtesy Steve Wampler)

SECRETS OF SUSTAIN

- **Neck/body joint types**
- **Thickness of the body and its relation with sustain**
- **Special fretboards**

"If you are going through hell, keep going."

- **Winston Churchill**

What is "sustain"

A guitar its said to have a "good sustain" when its sound keeps going, long after a string has been plucked. Sustain is not a factor of design: it is an objective of it. It is an attribute of good quality guitars, as it reveals a good construction technique. In this chapter we will review both the factors that help sustain, and those fundamental for it.

Neck heel and guitar heel

The **neck heel** is the part of the neck that joins the guitar's body. At the heel, the back of the neck changes from its typical rounded shape to a flat surface. The neck heel fits more or less tightly in the so called *neck pocket* (a cavity routed in the guitar's body) to which it is either glued or screwed.

The **guitar heel** is the part of the body below the neck pocket. **Neck heel and guitar heel** form together the **neck/body joint** (except in the case of neck-through instruments, naturally).

Neck/body joint types

Let's consider the different ways to attach the neck and body together, and talk about the characteristics of each of these joints.

Set-neck

The neck is glued to the body. Also called "set-in neck", this is the method typically used by Gibson.

Potential problems: the routing of the neck pickup cavity may weaken the joint. Replacing a glued neck requires specialized intervention.

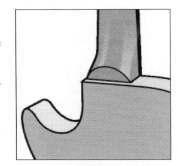

Bolt-on neck

The neck is attached to the body using screws. Advantages: neck replacement is easy.

Problem: because this type of joint is used on most cheap mass-manufactured guitars, all bolt-on neck guitars can be perceived as a low quality. But a correctly built bolt-on neck has a couple of pleasant surprises. Keep reading!

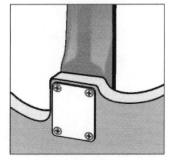

Neck-through-body

In this case there is no "joint" *per se* (no neck heel or neck pocket): the neck **extends right through the body of the guitar,** as a single piece of wood forming both the neck shaft and the body core. The lateral pieces of the body (called the wings) are then glued to this central core. Replacement is not possible without major surgery, if at all.

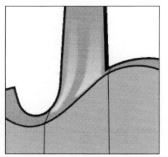

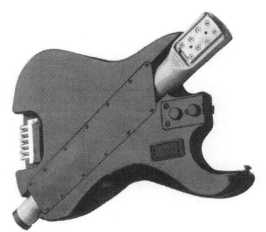

The Stow-Away™ model implements a clever neck mounting mechanism. More information on: www.stewartguitars.com.

Foldable or detachable joints

Some electric guitars feature a type of joint that allows the neck to be detached from the body. Sometimes the neck doesn't get completely detached, but folds on to the body by means of some kind of hinge. The most basic aspect of portability is simply *size*. Most bass cases are around 48" long (122 cm), but many airlines will allow you to take your instrument in the cabin only if the case does *not* exceed 46" (117 cm); otherwise it qualifies (and is charged) as bulk luggage. Package delivery companies (UPS, DHL, etc.) use a similar policy. An instrument need not have a detachable neck to be easy to carry and ship—sometimes all it needs is to fit into a case a couple of inches shorter!

A neck-dismounting mechanism normally adopts the form of a metallic plate which slides into a complementary piece on the neck pocket. Finally, some locking device (usually a thumb screw) will fix the neck in position. How will this resource affect sustain? It will normally be less stable than a permanent joint, but it shouldn't produce an audible difference as long as the mechanism effectively fixes the neck and the body together.

No joint at all

Some guitars are made from a single piece of wood. The myth of a supposedly exceptional sustain makes these guitars expensive, sometimes wildly so. Note that this is just a variation of the neck-through joint. My personal opinion is that building a single-piece guitar is not only a sub-optimal use of wood, but will produce an instrument with just average sustain, impossible to repair if the neck twists or bows. If you are building an instrument like a Chapman "stick", then using a single piece of wood is the way to go. But for me, reasonable justifications for building a normal guitar or bass this way are hard to find.

Joint type and neck pickup cavity

If the neck pickup cavity is routed too close to the neck pocket, the neck heel will simply not have enough wood around supporting it. The next figures illustrate the problem. In figure "A" the pickup cavity "eats" part of the neck heel (as it happens on Les Pauls, and particularly in SG's and Flying V's, which are set neck guitars with two cutaways). Figure "B" represents a bolt on neck, in which the pickup cavity does *not* intersect the neck pocket. Note that in both cases the neck pickup is placed at the same distance from the neck.

There are, however, two differences:

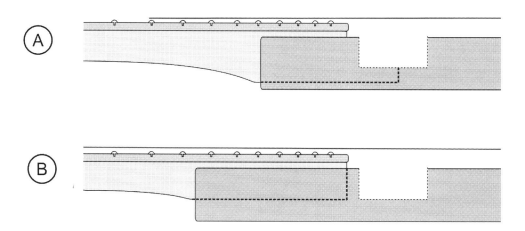

- The geometry of the neck heel and the guitar's body at the joint.
- The neck joins the body at different frets. Example "A" has a shorter heel, which has the benefit of allowing for a better reach of the higher frets, but the joint between neck and body has a smaller contact surface. In example "B", the neck joins the body 3 or 4 frets closer to the nut, so the playing hand will find the guitar's heel in its way sooner.

The common belief around *neck-through* guitars is that they sustain better than glued ones. And the myth goes on saying that *set-neck* guitars sustain better than *bolt-on* ones. I was very surprised to learn that according to research on the matter, things are exactly the other way around. The answer is provided by **R.M. Mottola** in an excellent article he wrote for *American Lutherie* magazine. He built a testing device (a single-string, neck-through body "guitar"), and measured the sustain using an electronic device. Then the neck was cut, and bolted to the remaining "body". A new set of measurements was taken. Finally, the neck was glued to the body, and again, sustain was measured, leaving all other factors constant (plucking force, components, even the wood was the same). All measurements were taken multiple times and averaged. The comparison parameter was the time (in seconds) during which the string kept vibrating from the moment it was plucked until the sound level descended to a predefined minimum. The results showed two interesting things:

1) A *bolt-on* neck actually sustains better than a glued one, and that a *neck-through-body* joint is the less sustaining of them all. Actually, the best performing type of joint was a bolt-on neck with a veneer of wood (a thin wood shim) between the body and the neck, to compensate for the material lost when the neck was cut from the initial neck-through-body configuration.

2) That difference in sustain is imperceptible in practice. It was in fact detected by digital signal processing software, but for the human ear there are no significant differences.

So, there it goes the "better sustain myth" of neck-through-body guitars. The valuable conclusion: building a good joint is far more important than choosing a particular type of joint. To our ears, it is a matter of the quality of the work. A perfect routing job is what a good neck-joint demands.

Joint type and guitar heel

The heel shape has an important role in playing comfort. To keep the player's hand from contacting a sharp edge, I like to build my guitars with a round-shaped heel. This offers better access to the higher frets, and I believe it adds to the beauty of the back of the instrument. In neck-thru-body guitars, the heel is not a problem, because there are no joints or screws in there; the neck flows into the body.

Thickness of the body

Now that we have discussed the interrelation between neck angle, guitar top, and hardware has been presented, we can finally discuss this topic in depth.

Body thickness of a guitar with bolt-on neck

The body must be thick enough to accommodate the electronics and the pickups, and offer structural support for the hardware and the neck screws. Stratocasters have a constant body thickness of 1 3/4" (45 mm—except on the arm rest bevel and tummy bevel, of course).

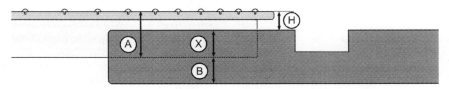

---

30 *Mottola, R.M. "Sustain and Electric Guitar Neck Joint Type", American Lutherie #91, 2007, p. 52.*

To define the **minimum** thickness of your bolt-on guitar's body, follow these steps:

1) **Decide** (or measure) the thickness of the neck's heel (marked Ⓐ in the graphic below).

2) **Decide** Ⓑ, the thickness of the heel. If it is too thin, it will affect sustain and weaken the joint; too thick, and the guitar might result too heavy and beefy. Suggestion: no less than 7/8" (about 22 mm) for a bolt-on instrument–maybe a little less for a set-neck guitar, and as thin as you like on a neck through body guitar. Ⓐ and Ⓑ must be consistent with the kind of body you are designing (light and thin? Heavy and thick? Something in the middle?)

3) **Decide** Ⓗ, the height from the guitar's top to the fretboard border. In angled-neck guitars, calculate this at the end of the fretboard (like shown in the figure above). For instruments with a flat top and Fender style bridge hardware, H *has* to be close to 3/8" (19mm) because of the height of the bridges used on such type of instruments..

The absolute **minimum** recommended value: as much as the *thickness of the fretboard + the height of the frets + about 5/64" (2 mm) of string action*, which should be a number around 5/16" (8 mm).

4) **Calculate** Ⓧ = Ⓐ - Ⓗ ; that is the depth of the neck pocket of your guitar–remember that for routing day. The thickness of your instrument at its thicker point is Ⓑ + Ⓧ.

Body thickness of a set neck instrument

An arched Les Paul top has a variable body thickness, ranging from 2" (50.8 mm) at the edge to 2 13/32" (61 mm) in the center of the body. For set necks of the Gibson variety that use a horizontal mortise and tenon joint, the Ⓐ, Ⓑ and Ⓧ measurements pertain to the thickness of the tenon, which can be just about any thickness in practice. So, the decision here must be made in function of Ⓗ, the distance between the fretboard and the guitar's top, which in a Les Paul is as big as the height of the fretboard's binding, so Ⓐ = Ⓧ . But of course, it doesn't necessarily have to be so.

So, what is the practical way to decide the body and the tenon thickness?

Follow these steps:

1) Establish the *minimal* body thickness in function of the control cavity, making sure it can be routed deep enough to accommodate all the electronics.

2) Note that in an angled neck, the guitar heel Ⓑ has a variable thickness. Make it thick enough to support the neck heel–in a Les Paul body, it is 3/4" at its thinnest point, at the edge of the body.

A set-neck ready to get glued in place (photo courtesy www.harvesterguitars.com)

3) Decide Ⓧ, so Ⓧ + Ⓑ is big enough for the control cavity you will need, defined by the kind of electronic components you plan to use (remember the tall push/pull pots? Are you using those?) Remember, Ⓑ must be measured at the edge of the body.

4) Ⓐ should be equal or slightly bigger than Ⓧ. In the picture they are the same, as in Les Pauls. You can place the fretboard higher, but remember that you don't have much room for variation here–the strings cannot end up so high above the top as to not meet the bridge!

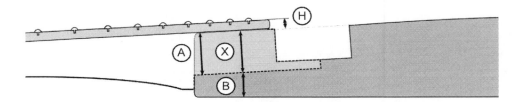

Body thickness of a neck through instrument

For neck through joint instruments, minimum body thickness is equal to the thickness of the neck core (the part of the neck that goes through the body).

The main variable to take into account is the necessary depth of the control cavity. Remember, if the instrument is too thin, you might not have not enough room to accommodate some electronic components.

A neck-through bass. The "wings" (the body´s laterals) can be seen attached to the neck's core.

Thickness of the body and its relation with sustain

It is believed that the more massive a guitar's body is, the more it will sustain. It could have less responsiveness, though. Customers who play improvisational styles may prefer a thinner instrument, which will sustain less but will react faster to the player's actions. This is an "empirical" generalization; as far as I know there is no research formally supporting these assertions. Plus, sustain depends on many other factors as well.

Thickness of the body and its relation with ergonomics

A thin guitar might feel more comfortable and lighter. It will leave less space for the electronics, though. However, some players like them heavy, sustaining and sturdy–discussing their preferences is a must.

Standard measurements–Body thickness

Explorer, Stratocaster, Telecaster, and Jaguars, Precision and Jazz Bass: 13/4" (45 mm);

Les Paul: 2" to 2 ^{12}/32" (50–61 mm); Gibson SG: 1 3/8" (35 mm)

Checklist

Designing a guitar with great sustain

The sustain of a guitar is strongly related to the neck geometry and setup. The joint, the frets, the neck material... all can contribute to a better sustaining instrument. Let's review the factors that influence the guitar's sustain.

First, the *guitar design* advice:

- **Forget the "neck-through" myth**. A bolt-on guitar will sustain as well as a neck-trough guitar, if not better. Neck-through construction can be more ergonomic, though: the neck just flows elegantly into the body. Also, the body can be thinner, and consequently, the instrument can be lighter–given that this is the preference of our customer (or ours).

- **The stiffness and quality of the wood is paramount**. Imagine you have a guitar made of latex and another made of marble. Which one will sustain better? Visit YouTube.com to see a couple of marble guitars in action [31]. Their sustain is endless. But few guitarists would welcome the idea of carrying a gravestone around, so use quality, stiff wood instead (not necessarily heavy wood–more on this in chapter 14).

- **Use "tall" frets.** Many Gibson Les Paul Customs, for example, were built with extremely low frets–higher ones will provide better anchoring for the fretted strings.

- **Choose a longer scale.**

And why not, some guitar making and guitar setup advice:

- **Maximize contact surface between the neck pocket and the neck's heel**. A neck pocket, cleanly routed, favors good vibration transfer.

---

[31] *Look for videos with the tag "stoneguitar" (one word).*

- **Avoid a loosely screwed neck**. It could damp the strings' vibration. Set those screws tight (without breaking them or the wood). *Tip:* applying the last half-turn of the screws with the guitar already stringed and tuned improves the body/neck contact.

- **File perfect strings slots at the nut and the bridge**. If the strings are well-seated in the slots, there will be less energy loss at those points.

- **Avoid action that is too low**. Low action is mostly desirable, but not to a point in which the strings hit the frets (even if the contact is not strong enough to create an audible buzz).

- **Set the height of the pickups correctly,** or else the pull of the magnets will "put the brakes" on the strings.

Part V

Parts, Materials and Finishing

13: Selecting the right hardware

This chapter compares different types of bridges, tuning machines, and nuts (all of them in contact with the strings and critical to guitar setup and intonation) and their compatibility with different body shapes, neck angles, and headstock types.

14: Selecting the right wood

This chapter is about the heart and soul of a guitar: the wood. It deals with aesthetical, qualitative and environmental concerns.

15: Selecting the right finish

In this chapter we review different finishing materials and their corresponding techniques, comparing their difficulty, risks and costs. We also review some classic finishing effects, and how to choose and combine colors.

*The parts you choose for your instrument will have
a deep impact on the function and on the visuals.*
(Photo: Dieter Stork - Instrument: "Sauron" - www.lospennato.com)

SELECTING THE RIGHT
HARDWARE

- **Bridges: types, compatibility, adjustment**
- **Nuts: types, materials, matching with bridge type**
- **Tuning machines: relation, anatomy**
- **Pickguards, form and function**

"I'm tired of being around men all the time. I'm going to start a band called 'Skirt' with three girls and I'll play the guitar and sing backing vocals in drag. I went window shopping when I was in New York; saw a lot of amazing dresses. "

–Brian Molko–songwriter, leader of the band Placebo

The basics

By the term "hardware" we refer to a number of parts, mostly made of metal: brackets, covers, plates, pickup rings, ferrules, screws, springs, strap buttons, string trees, retainers, etc. But the most important (and the subjects of this chapter) are the bridge, the nut and the tuners. They are the components that most strongly condition (and are conditioned by) the rest of the design. They are also the ones in contact with the strings, so they also have a role in the sound, intonation, setup, and playability of the instrument.

The bridge

The bridge fulfills three main functions:

- It sets the string length (and the so called "compensation", in most models).
- It sets the string spread and spacing.
- It sets the strings' action at the upper end of the fretboard.

In the next table, different types of bridges are related to different guitar bodies. A cross indicates incompatible or "unorthodox" applications (although not necessarily *impossible*).

Choice of bridge in function of the neck angle

Back in chapter 7 ("Neck design") we considered the relation between **neck angle** and **guitar top shape.** Now we analyze the relation between **neck angle** and **type of bridge** to be used.

In fact, neck angle, the guitar top shape and the type of bridge are elements that affect each other, and must be decided simultaneously.

See the next figure. An angled neck will require a high bridge, like the type of bridge mounted on posts. Otherwise, we end up with the strings placed too high above a low bridge (case **A**), not to mention the guitar's top and the pickups.

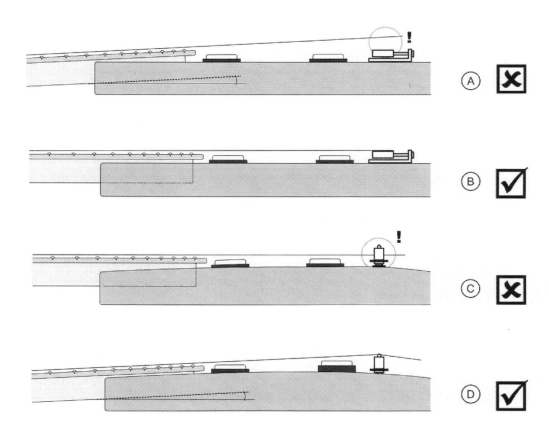

Combining a bridge designed for arch top guitars with a non-angled neck will cause the opposite problem: the strings lay too low in relation to the bridge (case **C**).

Cases **B** and **D** show the correct interaction between the angle of the neck and the type of bridge used. Other combinations may not work; see the following chart for a complete evaluation of the possibilities.

Bridge / guitar top compatibility chart

(**Reference:** ✓ = Usually OK ✗ = Usually not OK)

	On flat tops	On carved tops	On arch tops
Mounted on posts 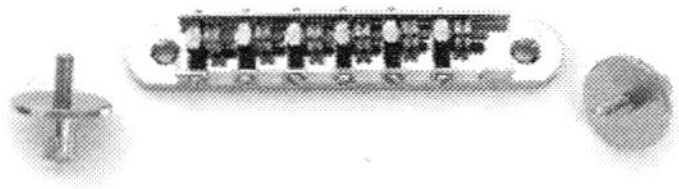	✗	✓	✓
Flat mount, screwed to the top 	✓	✗	✗
Mounted on posts on a wooden base 	✗	✓	✓
Tremolos (Floyd Rose, etc.) 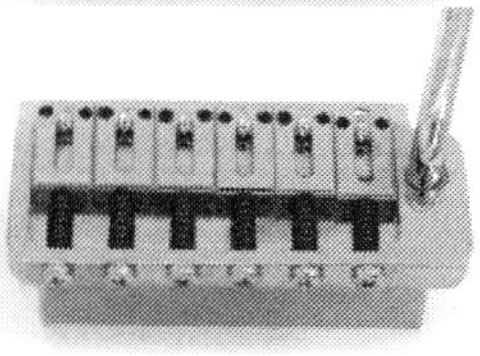	✓	✓	✗

The most important conclusions to draw from this chart are:

- **Install flat-bottom bridges on flat-top guitars with straight necks** (the keep-it-simple, Fender way).

- **Install post-mounted bridges on guitars with angled necks and carved top guitars, use bridges mounted on posts** (Les Paul style).

- In any case, **we need to know nominal heights** for these two types of bridges, for both guitars and basses. It will be necessary to measure it, or to check the bridge's specs, normally provided on the suppliers' websites.

Bridge adjustment capabilities

String length (intonation)

Imagine we build a guitar with absolute mathematical perfection; bridge and nut lay exactly at the same distance from the 12th fret: we've got ourselves a guitar that will never, ever, play in tune. The theoretical measurements do not work in reality as they do on paper. A fretted string is a *stretched* string, which slightly changes the vibrating length needed to obtain the note we wanted.

Compensation is a subtly complex issue, and falls beyond the scope of the design phase. Suffice it to say that each string saddle must be placed slightly *offset* towards the tail end of the instrument, than the pure mathematics dictate, to compensate for the stretch our fretting fingers impose to the strings. We are talking of just small fractions of an inch, which make the difference between a guitar that intonates correctly and a guitar that does not. As the amount of compensation varies with action, scale, string gauge, string quality, string materials, and probably also ambient temperature, a mechanism to adjust string length is desirable. The answer is to mount each string on individually adjustable saddles. Not all bridges provide individual intonation adjustments, though.

String height (action)

All modern bridges are adjustable in height; however, not all of them allow for *individual* height adjustment of each string. Some bridges can only be raised or lowered as a whole, which will work as long as the bridge radius is compatible with the fretboard radius.

String spread

This is a desirable adjustment capability that is not often present. Guitars produced in series don't need such flexibility in the bridge (they are manufactured after common, precise specifications) but custom instruments definitely do, to adapt to personal requirements of the player. If the guitar's neck is narrower or wider than the standard, then a string spread adjustment will be necessary to distribute the strings across the neck width and above the pickup's magnets. Some bridges without this feature come with un-notched saddles that provide for some amount of spread adjustment.

Bridge foundation

Bridges mounted on posts don't have full contact with the guitar's top. Since there are only two anchors, the bridge might not sit well—maybe it would if it were leaning on 3 points, the minimum required to completely limit the *degrees of freedom* of the piece (imagine that you are a photographer, and instead of a tripod, you have to take photos using a bipod). Some modern versions include a small screw that fixes the bridge to the posts, to avoid all rattle. However, the string tension is normally enough to hold down the bridge firmly in place. Flat-bottomed bridges have the whole base in contact with the top of the instrument. This is considered beneficial for both sustain and vibration transference, or at least such is many manufacturers' claim. I find this to be a contradiction, though: *sustain* and *vibration transference* are opposing concepts. A sustaining string will *not* transfer its vibration—it will retain it, to remain vibrating.

The advantage of a good foundation, though, is that it fixes the bridge completely; otherwise the bridge's own movement will absorb energy, reducing sustain.

The way the *saddles* (the individual bearing pieces on which the strings rest) are locked in place is a factor, too: on a number of flat bottomed bridges, the only thing holding each saddle in contact with the bridge plate is string tension.

Bridge adjustment chart

The fchart on next page shows the different adjustment possibilities discussed above.

	Length	Height	Spread	Tremolo	Tuning
Mounted on posts	✓	✓₁	✗	✗	✓₄
Flat base	✓	✓	✗	✗	✗
Tremolo	✓	✓	✗	✓	✗
Fixed Wrap-around	✗	✓₁	✗	✗	✗
Adjustable Wrap-around	✓	✓₁	✗	✗	✓₃
3D Adjustable	✓	✓	✓	✗	✗
Floyd Rose	✓	✓₁	✗	✓	✓
Headless	✓	✓	✗	✓₃	✓

✓ Yes   ✗ Usually no   ✓₁ Only whole bridge   ✓₂ Most models   ✓₃ Some models   ✓₄ with a special piece.

Micro tuning

You can use a bridge with micro tuners, or you can install an extra piece containing them that will also act as a tailpiece (compatible with non-tremolo, mounted-on-post bridges only). Floyd Rose's include their own micro tuners.

String anchoring

Some bridges provide string anchoring right on themselves. Other bridges have guide holes in the bottom of their bases, and for these you have to insert the strings from the back of the instrument. Post mounted (Tune-O-Matic) bridges use a separate tailpiece to anchor the strings - the *tailpiece*.

Tailpieces

The function of the tailpiece is to anchor the strings from the bridge side. The tailpiece also has an interesting effect on playability, which depends on how far from the bridge it is placed, and the resulting length of the strings from bridge to tailpiece. Such "tailpiece after-length" is more relevant to arch top guitar design; however, I find very interesting these paragraphs, from American Lutherie Magazine editor **Tim Olsen**:

> "Imagine two guitars with the same scale length, string gauge and action height. One is a shred Strat with a locking nut and bridge. The other is a jazz guitar with a long peg head and lots of string between the bridge and tailpiece. It takes exactly the same pull to bring a string up to pitch on each guitar–pitch is a function of string density, tension, and vibrating length, not total length–yet the two guitars will have a different playing feel. Why? Because strings are stretchy. If they weren't, they would just break and never come up to pitch. When the string is pushed to the fret, it has to stretch a little bit. The resistance you feel when fretting the Strat will be a function of the stretchiness of the vibrating length, plus the string between the nut and the tuning gear, plus the string between the bridge and the tailpiece. Those areas of the string outside the playing length form a sort of spring with extra stretchiness that makes the string feel less tight, so a heavier string can be used without the feel of the action becoming too stiff."

And he continues, discussing a conversation on the subject he had with the famous arch top guitar builder **Jimmy D'Aquisto**, in 1992:

> "[D'Aquisto] said that many makers, including his teacher John D'Angelico, had it all wrong when they made tailpieces which had the bass strings much longer than the trebles behind the bridge. Jimmy went to a straight-across tailpiece early in his career, and finally settled on a V-shaped arrangement where the E strings were the shortest. I asked him if this was not backward, considering the extra lengths at the peg head. He said no, the small wound G string should have the greatest total extra length".

(I have yet to find such "V shaped" tailpieces, though!)

(Photo courtesy of Tom Hollyer, www. es-335.net)

The art-deco tailpiece of the Gibson L-5. It contrasts in shape with the rest of the guitar, but it reinforces its classic character. One of the rare occasions in which gold- and silver-plated elements combine in a classy way. Form and function together, at its finest.

The nut

Nut functions

The nut has several functions, all critical to good intonation, sustain, and playability:

- It marks one end of the vibrating open strings, serving as a seating point for them.
- It leads the strings from the tuners to the fretboard.
- It sets the action at the lower end of the fretboard.
- In the case of compensated nuts, it contributes to the correct intonation of the instrument across the whole fretboard.

Nut materials

- **Bone**, which is the traditionally preferred material for making nuts. Its hardness and density contribute to good tone, it polishes well, and it allows for precise string slot filing. It is the material that other synthetic substances try to imitate or improve on (see below). Use a mask and eye protection when working with bone.

- **Thermoplastic** (generally just referred to as "plastic"). This kind of nut is used in low cost instruments; they tend to break often, to be damaged by string friction, and to kill sustain. Hollow plastic nuts are the worst option. Not recommended.

- **Tusq** is the brand name of a polymer which is claimed to reproduce the characteristics of bone, but at a lower cost and without bone's irregular pores.

- **Corian** is the brand name of a synthetic material made by Du-Pont and used for nuts. It is a non-porous material based on an acrylic polymer, which makes for a good nut material. Since it is available for many applications, it can be found on your local home improvement store in a variety of colors.

Different kinds of nut: a roller nut, a graphite nut, a locking nut, and a conventional one on this Les Paul.

- **Micarta** is the brand name of a composite made of paper and thermosetting phenolic resin. Softer than bone, but also very dense.

- **Metal,** normally brass, since aluminum would not resist the friction for long. It contributes to a brittle and clear sound. Common criticism: an open string (anchored on brass) and a fretted string (anchored on flesh and fret) may produce some tone issues. Plus, working with metal is always more difficult than working with plastic or other materials.

- **Ivory** was used in the past in high end instruments, but it's now *démodé* because of cost and environmental reasons (to get ivory, elephants or walruses must be killed). Do not use ivory–it is illegal in most parts of the civilized world (and where is not, it should be), it is expensive, it is difficult to find, it will not save a bad guitar, and it is just not right. Go for fossil materials, instead.

- **Fossil.** Nuts are available made of fossilized bone of mammoths, animals which have been extinct for some 30,000 years. Making a nut out of a prehistoric animal's petrified bone requires work though, and it isn't cheap. Polished fossil nuts can be very pretty, though. Use eye protection and a mask when working with them.

- **Graphite.** These nuts are made not of pure graphite, but of a polyester graphite fiber composite. The fiber has high tensile strength, but is quite soft to abrasion (in fact, any abrasion resistance of the graphite is due to the polyester, no to the graphite) which makes it easier to file the nut slots. It is also slippery, and the strings can glide with ease through the slots. That is important in guitars with tremolos to help reduce string breakage and improve intonation. It is also a hard material, which favors sustain.

Nut types

- **Plain nuts,** made of the materials described above.

- **Locking nuts**: some tremolo systems (like the Floyd Rose) require a nut that clamps the strings, to avoid detuning. The strings get stretched only from the bridge end. Locking nuts are fixed to the neck using screws, which can weaken the neck/head joint.

- **Compensated**: they shorten the length of each string in a precise way, to match the compensation at the bridge, improving the intonation across the whole fingerboard.

- **Roller nuts**: to reduce friction at the nut when the string is fretted or tuned or slackened with the tremolo, some Fender models feature nuts with small rollers or even two small metallic balls, on which the string can slide freely.

- **Zero fret:** instead of a nut, some instruments have a so called "zero fret", which is

A guitar with a nut and a zero fret. Note how deep the nut slots are: they act as strings guides and a retainers. (Photo: Roadside Guitars).

a bit taller than the rest of the frets and it is located at the nominal nut position. All the strings rest right on the zero fret. Proponents of zero frets claim advantages in consistency between open string and fretted string tone, because the open strings are in effect fretted, too.

Tuners

Already discussed in regard to their placement, here we will review them more in detail.

Tuner anatomy

The figure shows the components of a tuner, to which we will refer in the next sections.

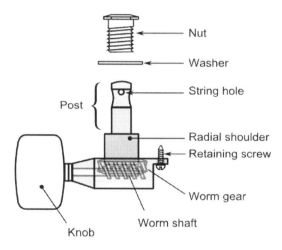

Tuner function

The tuners (also called "machine heads", "tuning machines", "tuning pegs"), have the function of regulating the string tension, so the strings can be taken to the correct pitch.

As with the rest of the hardware (except maybe the nut), tuners are things you don't design: you choose the ones best suited to your project (i.e., you buy them).

Turning ratio

It is the turning relation between the tuner's *knob* and the tuner's *post*. A violin's tuner has a 1:1 ratio— there are no gears, so *one* turn of the tuning peg results in *one* winding of the string around the post. A common tuning machine turning ratio is 16:1, which means that you have to turn the knob 16 times around to make the post turn once. The higher the turning ratio, the more precise the tuner.

Steinberger *gearless* tuners have an astonishing ratio of 40:1—they use a screw-like mechanism that pulls the strings in a straight fashion, eliminating winding. Micro tuners have a ratio of to 70:1, so small that they can only work as complement of regular tuners.

Tuner quality

A low quality tuner will present, sooner or later, one of the following problems:

- The tuner's knob becomes too hard to turn, because of lubrication or gear problems.
- The tuner's knob and post are not stable, but wobbly.
- The tuners will simply not maintain tuning of the strings.

Special types of tuners

Locking tuners. They have a mechanism that blocks the gear, providing a more stable intonation when used with heavy tremolo.

Bass tuners. They are special because of their size. They have to hold thicker strings wound around them, which put the machines under significantly higher tension. They have a wider knob, with more torque, and also have larger diameter posts.

Pickguards

Many instruments (guitars, more often than basses) feature a flat piece of plastic, wood or other materials, placed under the strings: the pickguard, also known as *scratch plate*.

As indicated by its name, the main purpose of the pickguard is to protect the guitar's finish from being scratched by the guitar pick. But it also:

- **Serve as a mounting base for the pickups and the electronics.** That was a very clever idea first implemented in the Stratocaster, making the production process more efficient: the woodworking and the electronics can be manufactured simultaneously, and assembled at the end of the production line. This design also simplifies repairs to the wiring once the pickguard is removed.
- **Fulfill an important aesthetic role**. Their shapes complement and emphasize some lines in the design. They can provide a touch of color, or contrast, or add a different texture to balance the whole. In some cases, they become a key element of the instrument's "personality".

Pickguard materials

While custom pickguards are made from a variety of materials, most manufacturers use various plastics, like vinyl, PVC, and acrylic. Other materials not frequently used nowadays are Bakelite, and celluloid, which is extremely flammable, and which tends to shrink over the years, developing cracks.

Expensive guitars may have luxury pickguards made from exotic woods, furs, skins, gems, precious metals, mother of pearl and abalone pearl.

Fastening

Pickguards are usually screwed to the guitar's top (Strats), which works well on flat-top instruments (and even maybe on guitars with cylindrical tops). But they will not fit a *domed* surface without getting distorted.

On a carved top guitar, plan for a pickguard mounted on special hardware, instead–like in a Les Paul. This design allows for a height adjustment to suit the guitarist's playing position, especially if this involves resting one or more fingers on the pickguard (also called a "finger rest").

If your instrument will have a pickguard, take advantage of the opportunity to reinforce the style of your instrument. It is one of those elements where form and function can meet marvelously well.

Checklist

Choosing bridge and nut

- **Match bridge type, guitar's top and neck angle.**

- **Match the fretboard and bridge radiuses.** A 3D-adjustable bridge will allow for a precise setup without need of modifications. A fixed-radius bridge (like a Tune-O-Matic) might need to have its saddles filed, so the strings follow the fretboard surface in a parallel fashion.

- **Decide the string anchoring.** Will you need a tailpiece? Will you use a bridge with string anchoring capability? Will you drill the guitar's body and use ferrules?

- **Fixed bridge, or tremolo?** Fixed bridges are easier to install. Tremolos require additional routing. Intonation is easier to keep on a fixed bridge, but the strings will have to be bent using your fingers only—which is okay if you happen to be more of a bluesman who doesn't care to design a **Steve Vai** *Superstrat*.

- **Do you? Care about designing a Superstrat, I mean.** Then combine the Floyd Rose bridge with a locking nut (they come often in a set). Be ready to drill some holes in the headstock joint; hopefully, you designed your guitar's neck with a volute, otherwise that long, 6-in-line, angled headstock it will be broken in no time.

- **Intensive string bending or tremolo use?** Go for a graphite or roller nut. The strings will last longer due to the reduced friction, which will also help in keeping the instrument in tune.

Choosing the tuners

- **Go for quality.** A guitar is about making music, and music is about musical notes. If the instrument looses intonation because of a mediocre tuner, the instrument cannot fulfill its mission.

- **Gearless tuners** offer an unbeatable tuning precision; however, the plain strings (G, B and E) must have a steel or silk wrapping at the tuner's end, otherwise they will detune during severe string bends. Consider also that the tuner's body is delicate; over-tightening will break it.

- **Some guitar tuners (and all bass tuners) have an axial hole inside the string slot in**to which you may insert the string end before you start wrapping around the post. This is elegant and will avoid having stingy, sharp string ends hurting your fingers.

- **Order the tuners correctly, according to your guitar's configuration.** If you designed a guitar with a 3+3 tuner distribution, make sure that you buy 3+3 tuners.

- From an aesthetic standpoint, choose tuners that are in harmony with the guitar's style; consider the material of the knobs, a vintage or modern look, etc.

(Photo courtesy of Ethan Prater)

SELECTING THE RIGHT
WOOD

- **Wood and its relation with sound**
- **Wood grade, price, and weight**
- **Biohazard and ecology**
- **The 4 laws of wood selection**

[MILES] (Explaining Jack how to taste a cup of wine):

Now, stick your nose in it. Don't be shy; really get your nose in there. Mmm... A little citrus... maybe some strawberry...

[Smacks lips] ... passion fruit...

[Puts hand up to ear] ... and, oh, there's just like the faintest soupçon *of like asparagus and a, just a flutter of a... like a... nutty Edam cheese.*

[JACK]: *Wow. Strawberries. Yeah. Strawberries. Not the cheese.*

[MILES]: *Are you chewing gum!!??*

–From "Sideways"–film by Alexander Payne, USA, 2004

Expert wine tasters are said to be able to sense more than 150 different aromas in wine.

Are there guitar experts, who can *hear* the wood? Is it true that mahogany has a "warmer" sound, and maple has a "brighter" tone?

While most guitar companies make such claims on their advertising, this is what independent researcher **R.M. Mottola** has to say in this regard:

"It may come as a surprise to a number of musicians that there is no definitive research showing any kind of correlation between wood species or basic construction

techniques used in electric guitars and particular tone coloring. My advice here is to pick materials that you like (for whatever reasons) and not to worry so much about how this may affect the sound. Paying attention to the ergonomics and weight of the instrument will be far more fruitful." [33]

For some traditionalists this might sound close to heresy. Granted, wood has an effect on the sound qualities, but let's remember that in an electric solid body instrument:

- **Such influence is subtle (**if not imperceptible!).
- **Such influence is relative.** As discussed in the past chapter, there are other factors that affect sound in a far greater way: pickups, amps, effects, electronics, and even the guitar cable.
- **It is *non-regressive* from sound to wood**. It is not possible to say what wood species a guitar is made of, just by listening. Some good quality guitars are made of synthetic materials; maybe it is impossible to say, only by listening to it, whether a guitar is even made of wood at all!

Example: Imagine a bolt-on guitar with a maple neck and a mahogany body. The brightness of the hard maple will interact with the warmth of the dense mahogany, in order to produce a more or less balanced tone. We hope. But if the maple neck goes *through* the body, the tone could get brighter. Or not. The maple would transfer more high overtones, but a neck-through construction transfer *less* highs. The point is: lutherie is not an exact science.

I have recently read this question a player posted on a guitar forum: *"I am going for Korina wood. Which pickups will better complement that wood? How do I get the 'Korina tone'?"*

Another member of the forum expressed his confusion. *"Is there a 'Korina tone'??"*

My favorite answer was given by a third member, in the form of an ironic slogan: *"Korina tone: strong and punchy low end, sparkly highs and a slightly pronounced mid-hump.*™ *"*

True, wood is a key aspect of musical instrument design and building. But looking for pickups to "complement the sound of the wood" is putting the cart before the horse.

Let's review the most important, objective characteristics of wood, instead.

Wood grade

The grade of the wood is a rating given to a piece of wood, based on the number, location and size of defects in the board, and the beauty of the figure.

High grade ratings identify, among other things:

- **Accidents:** pieces without knots, splits, checks, nail holes, fungi, etc.
- **Figure:** pieces with visible flame, or a specific quality of grain pattern
- Evenness of grain
- Evenness of color
- Evenness of figure

There are no universal systems of wood grading for lutherie applications. The highest hardwood grade in

---

[33] http://liutaiomottola.com/faqs.htm

the US is "FAS", which means "Firsts and Seconds". For the most part, when you buy ungraded wood from a luthier supplier (that is, when no particular grade is indicated) that is what you get.

Lutherie suppliers generally sell ungraded wood for use in building necks and solid body guitar bodies. Mahogany, alder, ash, maple and other common species used for necks and bodies are generally sold this way.

Luthier suppliers do provide visual grading for figured and other nice looking wood. This grading is highly un-standardized. There are three common grading "systems" (this is between quotes because none of these constitute any kind of system):

- From A to AAA (where AAA is the highest grade);
- From A to AAA, plus a "master grade" or some such;
- From A to AAAAA

Although it is always true that the higher the grade the higher the price, there is absolutely no uniformity to this grading system across different vendors and even across time for a given vendor. The only way to know what any vendor's rating system means is for the vendor to tell you. Some vendors are very good at this, most are not. Experienced luthiers buy their wood wherever they find what it is they want, but beginners are well advised to stick to vendors that specifically supply luthiers.

Wood price

Some of the variables affecting the price of wood are:

- First and foremost, the figure. Color, flame, and other visual characteristics are what make each wood piece unique.
- Availability (often related to ecological issues).
- Geographical situation of the buyer in relation to the origin of the wood. For example, a piece of lacewood would be much cheaper in Australia, where it comes from, than in Europe.
- The particular currency exchange situation between the point of origin and the point of sale.
- Dimension and geometry of the piece: size, flatness, thickness, etc

Wood weight

It is commonly assumed that a heavy, hard wood will contribute to better sustain than a lighter one. But, in fact, some lighter woods have been proved to sustain better. Why is that? Because sustain is related to stiffness, and not necessarily to the wood's density. Density alone will not do the trick.

Density might not affect the sound much, but it will affect the guitar's weight. A Strat body has a volume of about 3.3 liters (yes, I have submerged a Stratocaster body in water just to find this out). So, if you use alder wood, which has a density of 0.41 (it weighs about 410 grams per liter) the body will weight 1.35 kilos (a little over 3 lbs.). But a body made of *lignum vitae*, will weight around 5 kilos (11 lbs.). *Lignum vitae* has a density of 1300 grams per liter: it doesn't even float. Some like them heavy, but holding a 7 kilogram (15.5 lb) guitar for a couple of hours on stage would cause back pains even in a Terminator.

Biohazard

Some time ago I was tempted to experiment with alternative woods, and spotted a nice blank of *teak*, to build a bass. Teak is used on high quality furniture, those beautiful, modern Danish pieces. Fortunately, before I bought the wood I found out that teak is *bio-active*: it produces toxic chemical components, probably as a defense against insects.

On other occasion, I read an interview with a recognized classical guitar maker; he was asked which wood species he would use to build Spanish guitar sides, considering that the supply of Brazilian rosewood was so scarce. *"Quebracho",* he said, a species that I happen to know well since is native from the zone in Latin America in which I spent my younger years. It is an *extremely* hard and heavy, deep red wood. Beautiful. But quebracho can cause nasopharyngeal cancer, too.

The toxic effects are commonly transmitted by the dust; always use a protecting mask for nose and eyes. Even if you work with non-toxic species, the dust will cause problems in the long run, like loss of taste and olfactory senses.

A word on ecology

Aren't we damaging the environment, tearing trees down to make guitars? Should we abandon our guitar making work and do something else?

Of course not. Using wood is not anti-environmental. Using *some* wood is. Particularly in the case of lutherie there is an overuse of ebony, bubinga, wenge.... all at risk of extinction—clear and present danger of disappearing from the face of the Earth, forever.

We must squarely refuse to work with endangered species. Forget all the stories about this or that sound because of this or that wood; it is just marketing stuff. The advertiser himself could never differentiate between the sound of two identical guitars, one made of Madagascar rosewood and the other one made of ash. Nature will know the difference, though, since Madagascar rosewood is endangered and ash is abundant. Flamed maple, and many other top-grade, extremely beautiful and acoustically excellent woods are not at risk, as I write this.

The usual excuse

Granted, in classical and acoustic guitars the wood does play a defining role in sound. Is that an excuse for makers of acoustic instruments to use species at risk? Of course not.

When discussing this matter, there is a typical excuse that almost never fails to arise*: "if I don't do it, somebody else will".*

To begin with, an instrument made with endangered woods will be much more expensive, damaging its price/quality balance. On the other side, doing business in an ecological way is becoming a winning marketing strategy. If others make instruments with endangered species, why don't you advertise that your guitars are made exclusively with woods extracted from well-managed forests? If you work with suppliers and woods certified by the FSC (the Forest Stewardship Council), you can be sure of that assertion. [34]

Sometimes the excuse takes interesting forms: *"Cheap wood should be used for chairs. I am making musical instruments here".* So what? If we are professionals (or just human beings with a sense of responsibility) we better conduct ourselves as such; ethical concerns are a good starting point.

---

[34] www.fsc.org

The paradox of the forests

Have you heard about the "paradox of the forests"? It says that "the best way to stimulate forest renewal is the exploitation itself". As wood becomes a more requested product, reforestation becomes good investment. "The market will take care of it", they say.

There are two problems I see with this reasoning. First, exotic woods come from underdeveloped countries, where no environmental policies are in place to protect the natural resources, and where any local environmental law loses any chance of being remotely applied due to governmental corruption. Areas equivalent to many football fields disappear each *day* in the Amazon to illegal (or legal but corrupted) forestry. And nobody cares about the reforestation, afterwards. If it were up to these guys we would end up in a few years building guitars made of recycled-polycarbonate, or something like that. Their only concern is how to make a profit sucking up the natural resources.

Secondly, in those places where reforestation does indeed take place, the ecosystem gets destroyed anyway. Eliminating trees means eliminating all birds, insects, bacteria, mammals, and whatever else lives on and around them. Replacing those trees with a very geometrical plantation of new trees doesn't replace the preexisting ecosystem; what remains is a sort of a *desert of trees*. [35]

The 4 laws of wood selection

So, which species of wood should we use to build electric guitars?

- **Law #1:** Always select non-endangered species.
- **Law #2:** Choose species with minimal or null biohazard risks, as long as Law #1 is respected.
- **Law #3:** Go for species traditionally used in lutherie, as long as Law #1 and #2 are respected.
- **Law #4:** Use local species, as long as all the previous laws are respected. It will reduce contamination due to transportation and it will contribute to your local economy [36].

Wood deserves our respect, because it comes from a living thing. A piece of wood is not a piece of rock, glass or plastic. It is much more than that.

Let's use certified wood. Let's use it wisely. Let's minimize waste. Let's refuse doing business with exploiters, because that way we endanger ourselves.

---

[35] *"Plantations are not forests"* - http://www.wrm.org.uy/plantations/material/text.pdf

[36] *For a list of the woods most used in electric guitar making (complete with descriptions and physical data) refer to Appendix B.*

SELECTING THE RIGHT
FINISH

- **Types of finishes–Pros and cons**
- **Finishing techniques and effects**
- **Color: symbolism, associations, combination**

"The secret of Stradivari was lost when the chemist that sold him pine resin mixed with outhouse droppings in a jar went out of business 300 years ago."

–From American Lutherie–Author Unknown

Finishing is the last step before you put all the parts together, but it is the first thing anyone notices on a guitar. Here at the design phase, we are interested in **deciding which type of finish we want for our instrument,** regarding type, colors, and effects.

A professional finish requires a lot of practice and care, and it takes a lot of time to do. Plus, each finishing technique involves different materials, equipment, safety measures, and precise steps to be followed (a general outline of which is listed below). A good book on the subject is, in consequence, an indispensable companion to undertake the process, as the complexity of it clearly transcends the scope of the design phase [37].

The material offered here must be understood as a review and analysis of the options we have, and their basic characteristics, to decide which alternative is the most adapted to our design in terms of complexity, equipment needed, cost, potential hazard, and results.

---

[37] *I recommend "Guitar Finishing Step-by Step", by Dan Erlewine and Don McRostie, on which I based some of the information presented here.*

Types of guitar finishes

There are three basic groups of finishes, considering the way in which the finishing material "cures" ("dries", becoming solid):

- **Evaporative.** Solvents evaporate and allow the suspended resin to return to its solid state. Typical evaporative finishes used in lutherie include **lacquer, shellac** and **spirit varnish.** An important quality of evaporative finishes is that subsequent coats burn into the coats previously applied, to form a single mass. This makes rubbing and buffing easier. Of these, only lacquer is generally used for electric guitars.

- **Reactive.** They cure either by a reaction with oxygen in the air, or by the action of a hardener added just before application. Examples: polymerized **oil, polyester, and 2-part polyurethane finishes**. **Oil varnish** and **gel finish** (a gelled form of oil varnish) also belong to this group. Polyester and other 2-part finishes are commonly used in commercial electric guitars.

- **Coalescing.** The evaporating component is water, allowing the suspended components in the finish to "coalesce" (unify), sticking together and forming a film on the surface. In this group we find the **water base lacquers**. These are often used by small electric guitar shops.

Steps of guitar finishing

Depending on the type of finish, materials and effects you choose, more or less of the following steps will be required. Some of them are iterative; others (like sanding) need to be performed at several different points of the finishing process.

- **Surface preparation.** Filing, scraping, sanding, clean off contaminants and residues from the wood (like silicones, wax, dirt, etc.)

- **Repairing imperfections.** Chips, dents, tear outs, holes and other accidents are filled with a particular type of product, depending if the top finish is clear or opaque.

- **Sealing.** This step can also be done before the color coats are sprayed. The goal is to seal the grain so color from subsequent applications does not bleed into the grain of the wood.

- **Grain filling,** to achieve a smooth surface on wood with large pores.

- **Sanding** using progressively smaller *grits* (the grit indicates the coarseness of the sandpaper).

- **Masking,** in case the instrument has binding or it has to be painted with more than one color, or to cover surfaces not intended to receive finishing (for example, the neck pocket).

- **Applying a primer layer of base paint**, to ensure that successive layers will stick to the surface (this is relevant only when applying opaque finishes).

- **Color spraying.** This phase also involves applying and creating effects, if that is the case. Examples: sunburst finishes, crackled finishes, airbrushed finishes.

- **Spraying of transparent coats.** They protect the color and "build" the layer that will be buffed and polished.

- **Buffing,** using a buffing machine and different compounds. This requires expertise, which is normally acquired after burning finishes to the bare wood. It is a process in which accidents can happen, too. The guitar can get caught by the fast-rotating polishing wheel and violently thrown in your face. Use a full mask.

• **Polishing**. Using creams or liquids, applied by hand.

Finishing Materials

This section presents the finishing materials most used on electric guitars. Descriptions include a brief comment on the **equipment needed** to apply the material, **toxicity**, the **gloss level** that can be obtained, and how adapted it is to first time guitar builders.

Glossier doesn't mean *better*–it depends on the visual effect you want to achieve with the finish.

Nitrocellulose lacquer

This is an *evaporative* finishing material, according to the categorization above. Relatively easy to use, dries fast and hard, and buffs to a high gloss. This is the traditional finish of electric guitars. It was used exclusively by commercial manufacturers until relatively recently. The finish is sprayed on. Highly toxic for you and for the environment. It can get easily damaged when in contact with certain synthetic substances (found in guitar stands, hangers, or even cases).

An important investment in equipment is necessary to apply nitro finishes professionally, but the practical advantage for the first timer is that it can be applied used spray cans, too.

Oil finish

Oil is a *reactive* finishing material. Much easier to apply than other finishing methods, if done properly it can result in a beautiful enhancement of the wood figure. Typical oils include Tung, Linseed and what are generally referred to as "Danish" oils. The finish is applied by hand, using a rag. Sometimes it is not considered a "professional" finish, particularly on guitars, but on basses it is pretty commonly used.

Finishing with this method involves sanding and applying a polymerized oil many times, until the surface of the wood has a smooth and natural feeling.

It will not polish to a high gloss, though: it will stay matte or semi-matte. This is specially adapted to first time builders, since it is a cheap, easy and quick process compared to all others presented in this chapter.

---

[39] *The most complete information I have found on the subject is the book "How To Create A Factory Guitar Finish With Just A Couple Of Spray Cans!", by John Gleinicki. It also includes access to online clips describing the process. Visit* www.paintyourownguitar.com.

Polyester and polyurethane

These are reactive finishing materials. This is the kind of finish used by the automotive industry and by most large guitar manufacturers today.

Advantages: it produces a hard, thick, high gloss finish. It builds quickly and the buffing process is relatively easy.

Disadvantages: it requires extremely toxic hardeners to cure, it is extremely flammable (and explosive!), and very expensive facilities and equipment are necessary. Polyester and polyurethane finish is definitely not adequate for beginners; these methods lie beyond what even more experienced luthiers can manage in a safe and economic way.

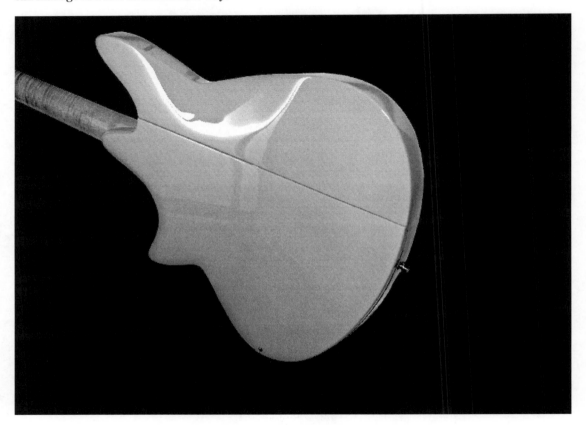

Water-based lacquers

Water-based lacquers are *coalescing* finishing materials. They have become increasingly popular with small builders, given the risk posed by other lacquer finishes in terms of flammability, health and environment. Water-based lacquers consist of microscopic particles of resin (acrylic or urethane, or a blend of both) suspended in a mix of solvents, water and other components. They are non-flammable. Solvent toxicity is the same as for other lacquers, but they are present in much reduced amounts in water-based finishes. Water-base lacquers need to be used with compatible products for pore filling, color shading, sanding, and buffing.

Although most builders are spraying the water-based lacquer, this product also works well as a brush-on finish, which makes it more adapted for the novice guitar maker. It can be applied with brush, which for the beginner is easier that using spray, but it may need a little more work to level the coats.

Other advantages in comparison to solvent-based lacquers is that water-based lacquers have a high solid content, so less quantity of the material is used to finish each instrument. It doesn't use solvent-based thinners, but distilled water or a compatible reducer. It can be shipped with almost no restrictions - unlike hazardous/toxic materials. Clean up is easier, using warm water.

French polish

French polish is an evaporative finishing process. Used on acoustic instruments, primarily classical guitars, it consists of the application of many thin coats of *shellac* (a resin secreted by a bug from the forests of India and Thailand) dissolved in alcohol and applied using a rubbing pad. The finishing material's name is "shellac", and the application technique is called French polishing. The rubbing pad is made up of wadding inside a piece of fabric, commonly referred to as a *muñeca* (Spanish for "doll").

Advantages: it results in a very high gloss surface, with a deep color and *chatoyancy* (the wood grain achieves a striking three-dimensional appearance); it is an excellent sealer, because it sticks to almost anything.

Disadvantages: although it is easy to repair, is highly sensitive to water, alcohol or any other liquids, including sweat. Precisely because of that, French polish is not normally used on electric guitars except for achieving a faster, non artificial aging process.

No finish

You can just leave the wood natural. Some players like the texture of the wood as it is. However, perspiration will stain and damage the wood, and the look is not at all professional. Not recommended. Go for oil, instead. It will protect the wood and look beautiful.

So, what is the best finishing method for me?

If you want an easy, quick, cheap and yet beautiful finish for your instrument, especially if it is a bass, apply an oil finish. It is ideal if you are working with minimal equipment and working space— possibly a small area or table at home.

If you want to achieve a high gloss finish and have spraying equipment and an adequate finishing room, use water-based lacquers. If you don't have the equipment, some water-based lacquer can be applied by brush, but you'll have to invest a little more time and attention during the rest of the finishing steps.

If you absolutely must have a nitro or polyester finish, send the instrument to a professional. They have the tools and the skills, and will deliver the best results. That is the most convenient way in terms of time, money, safety and results. The price of a professional finish of a guitar's body might be between $200 and $400. Buying the equipment and acquiring the skills do it yourself will only be financially justified after many instruments, if ever.

Worst case scenario: Application of all finishes requires excellent ventilation, wearing a respirator, protective gloves, and a place where the finish can cure without people around breathing the fumes. These products contain nasty chemicals that are absorbed through the skin, and stored in your liver—you don't want any part of that. Some finishes (polyester finish, for example) require compressors and ventilators which are enormous and expensive. The light switches and electrical

appliances used in the finishing room must be "explosion-proof", since a single spark might cause a disaster. If you want to install your own finishing workshop, the aid of a technical consultant with experience on this kind of equipment is indispensable.

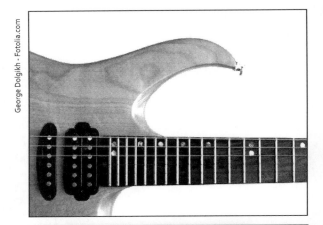

George Dolgikh - Fotolia.com

© Timothy Norcia - Fotolia.com

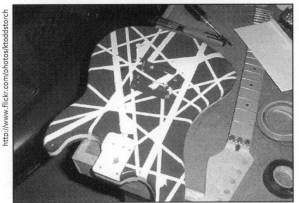

http://www.flickr.com/photos/ktoddstorch

Effects

Natural (transparent) finishes

Guitars and basses are conventionally finished in what we call "solid colors", which makes sense on wood pieces without any special visual appeal of their own. But if the wood figure is interesting, you may want to apply a transparent finish instead (either completely clear, or with a translucent stain). Lacquers or oils applied this way will bring out the full beauty of the grain, which makes this alternative a default choice for nicely figured woods. Make sure that all other products to be used (base, sealers, fillers, etc.) are also transparent.

Sunburst

At the center of the surface there is an area of lighter color (often showing the wood grain underneath) that darkens gradually towards the edges before hitting a dark rim. It can be formed by different colors (from yellow to orange, red and finally to black, for example), or by concentrations of one color, normally a stain that shows the grain of the wood in the center.

Patterns

Patterns and backgrounds are formed by repetitive abstract or figurative motifs. Examples are polka-dots, "Van Halen" stripes, or infinity of other possibilities. These effects require extensive use of masking, much care to avoid making a mess, and a very good job in applying the last lacquer coats to hide the imperfections between the different layers of color.

Color–A little theory[40]

Primary, secondary and tertiary colors

We can define *color* as a visual attribute of objects, derived from the spectrum of light (distribution of light energy versus wavelength) reflected by them. **Red, Yellow** and **Blue** are called "primary" colors as they cannot be obtained by combining other colors; in fact, *all* other colors can be derived as a combination of the primary colors.

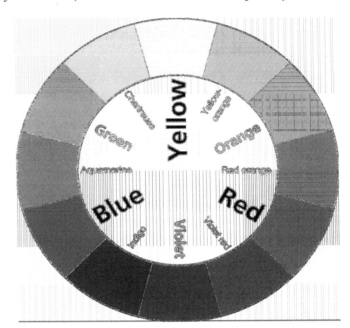

Secondary colors are those obtained by the combination of the primary colors, taken two by two. They are **orange** (red + yellow), **green** (blue + yellow), and **violet** (red + blue).

Tertiary colors are those obtained mixing a primary and a secondary color. They are:

- **red-orange,**
- **orange-yellow,**
- **violet-red,**
- *chartreuse* (yellow + green),
- **aquamarine** (green + blue),
- **indigo** (blue + violet).

Which colors combine?

The relationship among colors can be analyzed in a very practical way using a *color wheel*, which is an abstract, illustrative organization of color hues around a circle (figure on the left). The center is white, because white comprises all other colors in it (remember, we are making an *optical* approach to the subject; mixing paint from a lot of different cans will hardly produce anything close to white).

Combining adjacent colors produces all the intermediate hues. What's especially interesting about the color wheel is that it helps us *combine* two or more colors. For example:

- **"Analogous" colors** lay adjacent to each other on the wheel; they combine well because they are closely related. They blend well into each other.

- **Complementary colors** are located on opposing sides of the wheel. They contrast, enhance and intensify each other. Often it is a good idea to use a complementary color as the highlight color, and the other as the background. They can be eye catching, but sometimes they can be an eyesore, too. To make a contrast less evident, you can use a color not with its *direct complementary*, but with an analogous (an adjacent color) of that complementary.

---

[40] *This discussion avoids the complexity of "additive" and "subtractive" color theories, using only the conventional, "everyday" human perception as reference.*

● **Triadic colors** are those located 120° from each other. In some way, they are a "synthesis" of the whole wheel; for that reason, they are very "energetic". I have yet to find a pleasant-looking guitar or bass that uses color triads.

Color meanings and associations

The following chart shows different colors classified as "warm" or "cold". There is no complete agreement on which color belongs to which polarity; in principle there is an association with hot and cold things in nature (i.e., *blue frozen water* and *red hot iron*). Some of the psychological or cultural associations for the main colors are included, which can be useful to understand how the color harmonizes with the guitar user. Each color can have positive and negative associations:

Cold	Neutral	Warm	Mixed
Blue 👍 Importance, peace, intelligence 👎 Sadness, coldness	**Black** 👍 Seriousness, mystery 👎 Evil, death, darkness	**Red** 👍 Love, passion, heat, joy, power 👎 Anger, danger, rage	**Purple** 👍 Royalty, romance, sanctity 👎 Arrogance, gloom
Green 👍 Growth, health, environment, harmony 👎 Immaturity	**Brown** 👍 Earthiness, simplicity, friendliness 👎 Dirtiness	**Yellow** 👍 Happiness, joy, remembrance 👎 Cynicism, bad luck	**Lavender** 👍 Grace, elegance, delicacy, femininity
Grey 👍 Sophistication, Formality 👎 Dimness	**Beige:** 👍 Sobriety, relax, distinction 👎 Weakness	**Orange** 👍 Energy, warmth change, health 👎 Aggression	**Turquoise** 👍 Femininity, sophistication
White 👍 Purity, innocence, softness 👎 Coldness	**Silver** 👍 Glamour, wealth, richness 👎 Rigidity	**Gold** 👍 Extravagance, richness 👎 Falsehood	**Pink** 👍 Sweetness, love, playfulness 👎 Childishness

Source: see credits in page 2.

Incompatible colors

Combining colors is a matter of personal taste, but here you have some advice:

● Mixing warm and cold colors is a tricky business. Neutral colors go well with vintage style instruments, and serve well as background.

● Caution when using two or more primary colors. They combine well in race cars and toys, but not always on electric guitars. Primary colors are very powerful used alone, though.

- Dark on dark. Black goes well with everything, except with other dark colors. For example, think of a dark *navy blue* pickguard on a black guitar.

- Caution when using light on light. Very light colors can be confusing when used together. But white will generally combine well with any light color.

Each part of the guitar suggests a certain degree of "lightness" or "heaviness"–in *visual* terms. Light colors give a less substantial impression than dark ones. Brilliant colors visually weigh more than neutral colors in the same areas. Warm colors, such as yellow, tend to expand an area in size, whereas cool colors, like blue, tend to contract an area. And glossy areas seem to visually weigh less than matte areas. Take all these subtleties into account when deciding the colors of your instrument.

Look on the web for color palettes with harmonic color combinations. Combining colors is not only a matter of wavelengths or names–take advantage of the expertise of those specialized in creating and combining colors.

Checklist

From a design standpoint, in regard to finishing you have to decide:

- **The material to be used** (nitro? Polyester? Etc.), and the associated process. Think equipment, hazard, costs, time and difficulty vs. your skills and experience on that particular technique.

- **The opacity of the finish** (clear finish, stained, or opaque?) Use solid colors for unattractive wood pieces (made of basswood, for example), and transparent or stained finishes for wood with nice figure.

- **The color you will use.** Consider the instrument type, the player's gender, age, and music style, etc.

- **The effects you will use** (sunburst, crackled, or some other?) "No effects at all" is a perfectly valid choice, of course.

Additional advice:

- Choosing close grained wood (see details of different species on Appendix B), like maple for example, will simplify the process. Wood with irregular surfaces (open grain, splits like spalted maple) need much more work of filling, sanding, etc.

- Oil finishing is less messy and much cheaper than spraying, and it gives nice results. Not indicated for all kinds of wood, though (for example, lacewood). Try this method on basses, or any instrument with highly figured wood.

- **Again, the most important advice is**: Do it yourself only if you have the equipment, time, expertise, and facilities. Otherwise, have it done by a professional.

Finishing is the last step of guitar making; after weeks or months of hard work you want to see how the guitar looks already–but you can't until this step is done. And it is the longest, most difficult, messy, and most prone to mistakes of them all.

When finishing time comes, be patient!

(Photo: Danny Valdez)

... Or, you just can apply a broken mirror to the top, like in this Ibanez Iceman, and save yourself some time and money (just kidding).

Part VI - <u>Completion</u>

16: The blueprint of your new design

This last chapter explains, step by step, how to draw the blueprint of your guitar or bass, which will be the map you will follow when you build your instrument.

THE BLUEPRINT OF YOUR NEW DESIGN

"Without geography, you're nowhere."

- **(Unknown)**

The final step of designing a guitar or bass is drawing a complete blueprint, the map that will guide you during the construction phase.

As you will see on the next pages, the blueprint must include the following drawings:

- A front view of the instrument
- A side view
- A section view of the neck (at the 1st fret, and at the 12th fret)
- The wiring diagram

If you could follow only *one* piece of advice from this book, follow this one: **Do not start building your guitar without a well drawn blueprint.** You cannot build a good guitar just using guess work, or hoping to resolve problems as you go.

If you follow a second piece of advice, follow this one: **Make your blueprint real size** (scale 1:1). I am talking about the final version; to spare paper and effort, you will have to go through a few drafts before everything seems to work fine together. It is much easier to work on the drafts if they are made on regular-sized sheets.

Elements needed

For the final blueprint, you will need the same elements described in the introduction of this book (a mechanical pencil, erasers, and a short, transparent ruler), plus:

- **A long ruler**—28" long as a recommended minimum (700 mm or more). Use it to draw the strings and the fretboard sides, Avoid using a short ruler: the resulting straight line will not be straight at all. Errors of a fraction of an inch become enormous at the end of an ill-drawn line.

- **A protractor,** transparent if possible.

- **A few E size sheets of paper** (34" by 44") or ISO A0 size (33 7/64" × 46 13/16" or 841 × 1189 mm)—any smaller size will just not be big enough. Drawing in real size, you will just measure, transport and calculate drawing elements without painful scale adjustments. Plus, you will see the size of your instrument right there, without having to mentally calculate if it is too small or too big.

Drawing the blueprint using a computer

If you feel more comfortable drawing with computers, you can use one, of course—it's the professional way to do it. As discussed before, this will require knowledge of a suitable drawing software. At some point you will have to print your drawing in real size, though, which will cost some money.

How to draw the blueprint - Front view

Whatever the medium you choose, I propose following this sequence to draw your design:

1) **First, draw the axis of symmetry**. That is the base of the whole drawing:

2) **Mark the scale**, leaving enough space at each end to draw the body and the headstock later on.

3) **Mark the main dimensions:** Fret 0 (nut); 5th, 12th, and 24th frets; and bridge. The dotted rectangle represents standard guitar case dimensions—useful if you want to limit the size of your instrument to it for some reason (internal case spaces are not represented).

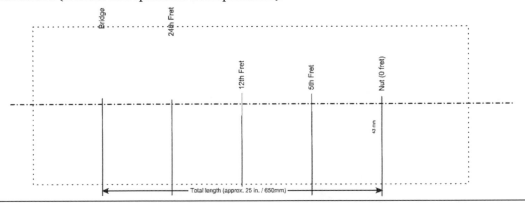

4) Draw the nut and the bridge in such a way that the scale end is placed on the bridge's *saddles*. Do not worry about compensation at this point; you will deal with it after the guitar is built.

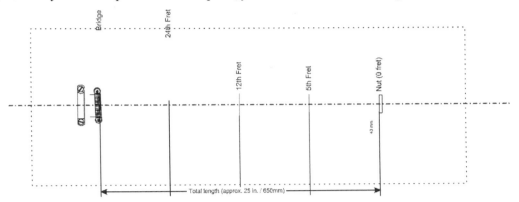

5) Mark the spread of the strings at nut and bridge. Draw the centerlines of the strings.

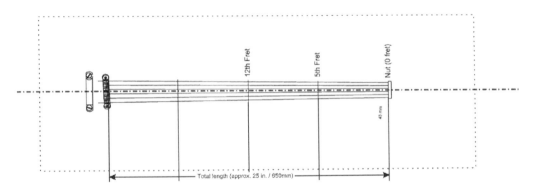

6) Draw the fretboard edges. Draw the end of the fretboard, too. Example: for 24 frets the distance from the nut to the end of the fretboard is 0.75 times the scale (fret 24) *plus* ⅓" - 8 or 9mm). On some other part of the blueprint, you can draw the neck section profiles, both at the first fret and the 12th fret. Detail the space for the truss rod pocket.

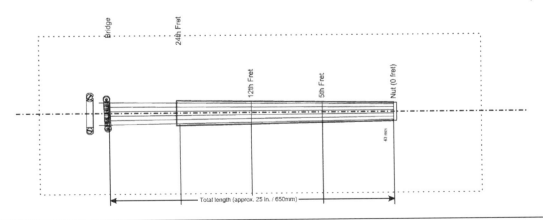

7) Draw the pickups, including pickup mounting rings (if used) and the pickup cavities.

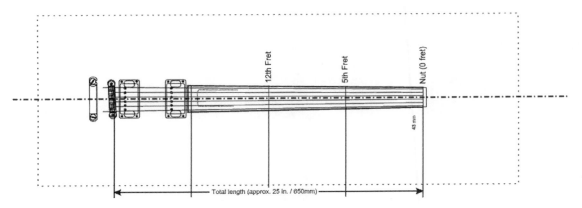

8) Draw the guitar's body.

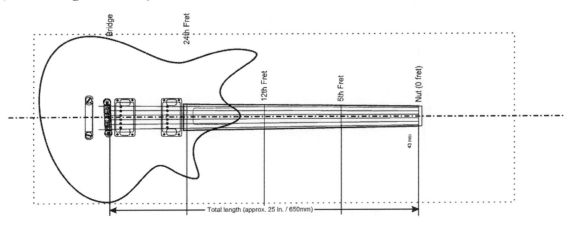

9) Draw the controls: knobs, switches, jack, etc.

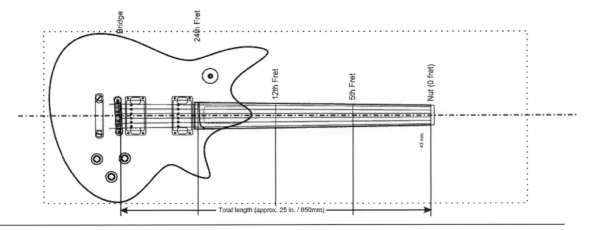

10) Draw the perimeter of the control cavity around the controls (not intersecting with other cavities, not too close to the border, not intersecting with the bridge). Draw the inset for the covers of those cavities. Draw any connecting channels and recesses (tummy bevel, arm rest, etc.)

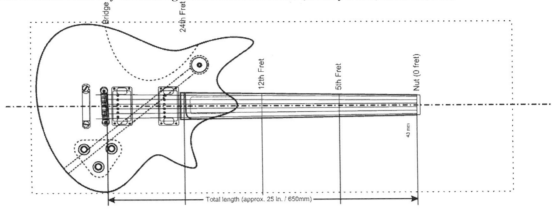

11) Draw the pickguard.

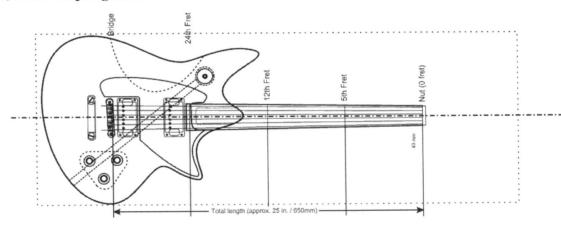

12) Draw the tuners.

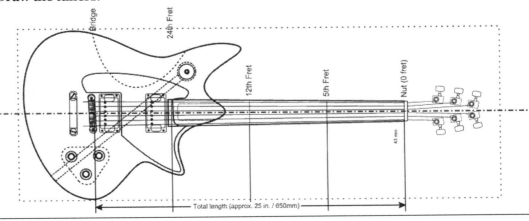

13) Draw the headstock perimeter around them.

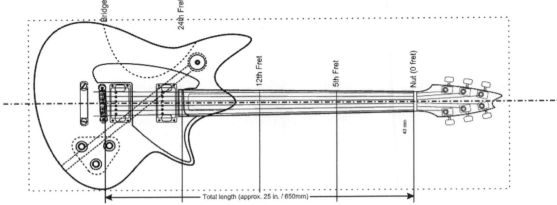

I haven't drawn the frets, in order to better appreciate the drawing of the neck/body joint, the truss rod channel, and the relation between strings and the edge of the fretboard.

The resulting front view drawing forms a series of outline templates: one for the headstock, one for the fretboard, and one for the body, the control cavity, the pickguard, and so on.

Side view

The top view drawing does *not* attempt to show any angles between headstock and neck shaft or neck shaft and body. It is a good idea to note this fact right on the drawing. So, using the top view as a reference, we need to draw a *side view*, describing the following elements: neck angle, headstock angle, cavities depths, internal channels placement, thickness of the instrument, joint dimensions (neck heel and guitar heel), the relation between fretboard and guitar top, and a side view of the neck (to see the neck thickness and volute placement).

Using the top view as a reference, follow these steps:

1) Draw the body. If the top of the instrument is arched, the longitudinal arching profile is drawn. The side view of the body is generally drawn orthogonal to the front view of the body.

2) Draw the neck pocket (it defines the neck angle).

3) Draw the fretboard and the neck. Pay special attention to the neck angle: if there is one, the side view of the neck and fretboard *cannot* be drawn orthogonal to the front view of same.

4) Draw the nut and bridge.

5) Draw the headstock and the volute. Again, **if there is** a neck or headstock angle, the side view of the headstock *cannot* be drawn orthogonal to the front view of same.

6) Draw the tuners.

7) Draw the pickup cavities, control cavity, and the controls.

At the end of the process, your blueprint will look something like the picture below (plus the neck profiles and the wiring diagram). The rectangle in the figure on next page represents an E-size paper sheet (34" × 44" ; 864 × 1118 mm), with a 39 ½" (100cm) long guitar draw on it.

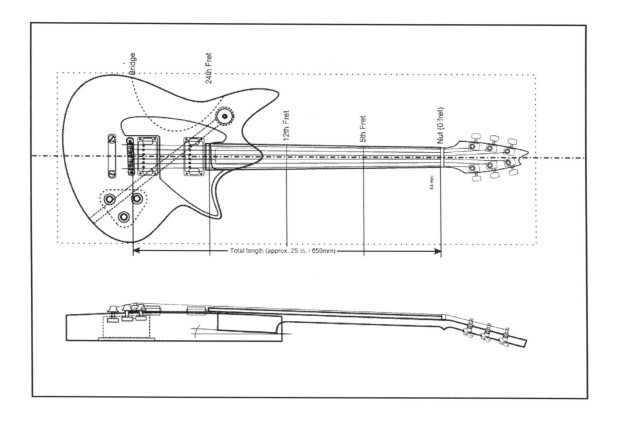

Wiring diagram

Draw the wiring diagram in detail on a separate, letter-size sheet. It will be easier to handle than a huge E-sized blueprint later on, when you are working on soldering the components. Draw the components in real size and distributed as they will be on the guitar–that will help you calculate the length of wire needed to connect them.

What to do with the blueprint?

- **Use it to build prototypes** (even if they are just cardboard models). Check the balance, sizes and proportions against your own size, for example in front of a mirror.
- **Use it to calculate the size of the wood pieces** you need to buy.
- **Use it to prepare a shopping list**.
- **Use it as a permanent reference during the construction phase.** The blueprint is your best friend during the guitar making process.
- **Use it to build the outline templates enumerated above.**

After you have the final version of the blueprint, pat yourself on the back: you just got yourself the complete design specification of your new electric guitar or bass.

Congratulations!

FAREWELL

"Don't worry about the world coming to an end today. It is already tomorrow in Australia. "

– Charles Schulz (cartoonist, creator of "Charlie Brown")

Clifford Stoll, American scientist and author, said: "The first time you do something, it is science. The second time, it is engineering. The third time, it's [just] technology".

And what is it called when you don't even do the thing yourself anymore, but a machine makes a million copies? Then it is not even technology. It is not even *doing*.

Not all making of musical instruments is *lutherie*.

It is not lutherie when materials get transformed on a production line into guitars which have hardly been seen by human eyes. That is merely a mass industrial process.

It is not lutherie when self-proclaimed high-end luthiers use wood coming from endangered species to produce "exclusive", "handmade", "master-built", "luthier-made", "unique", or "boutique" instruments. It is, at best, negligence.

It is not lutherie when a corporation invests millions in an advertising campaign announcing a so-called "new" model—which invariably turns out to be the same old model, only painted in some other color, or endorsed by yet another musician.

William Cumpiano, author and luthier, wrote:

> *Everyone wants to **be** something but nobody wants to **become** something.*
>
> *Everyone wants to be an expert but no one wants to become one. But you must become before you can be.*
>
> *I often find myself telling my students: "Drop your illusions. You cannot become a luthier after taking a course. You can pick up some mental tools and some knowledge about the assembly process. But not experience. You can only acquire experience, like you do age. Experience comes after many guitars".*
>
> *A master is someone who has made more mistakes than you, has made mistakes you haven't made yet, and has learned how to embrace them—thus learning to see them coming before they happen.*
>
> *So you go towards mastery one mistake at a time. How many mistakes can you stand? As many as it takes to be a master. The master has persevered past the errors until he's made all of them.*

From time to time newspapers announce that "the secret of Stradivari" has finally been discovered. As if making exceptional musical instruments were a matter of one single variable!

There is not *one* secret. There are many.

Let's *become*, and they will be revealed.

Thanks for reading!

Appendixes

A. Interviews

B. Characteristics of wood

C. Pickup color codes

D. Pickup cavities templates

Appendix A

INTERVIEWS WITH GUITAR DESIGNERS

I prepared three questions that summarize the main concepts of this book: **inspiration, sound, beauty, playability and originality,** and interviewed a few recognized designers in Europe and the United States. These are their answers. Enjoy.

Ned Steinberger

1) What inspires you? How do the ideas come to you?

Ideas come from pure thought, at any time of the day or night, and from experimentation, trial and error. In my case error has always been my best teacher. My inspiration comes from the challenge. I love to solve problems, and the possibility of doing things better, motivates me to try.

2) Playability, sound, and beauty: list them by importance

Is your heart more important than your liver or your brain? The way an instrument plays, the way it sounds, and the way it looks are all vital, and in my experience they all have about equal importance to musicians, although they might deny it. In my view, aesthetics impact sound and playability because the player responds philologically to his or her visual relationship with the instrument.

3) What makes your designs unique? What do you think is your differential against the rest of the world?

That's for others to say!

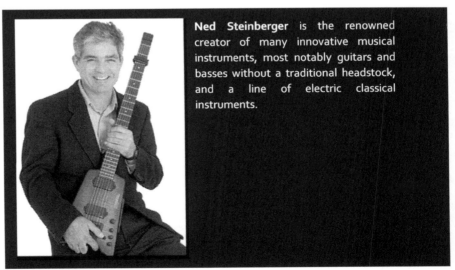

Ned Steinberger is the renowned creator of many innovative musical instruments, most notably guitars and basses without a traditional headstock, and a line of electric classical instruments.

R.M. Mottola

1) What inspires you? How do the ideas come to you?

My background is in engineering and so I take a somewhat formal approach to the design of electric instruments. In this context, the word design is rather interesting, as it means different things to different people. For engineers, "design" is a formal process of development to meet requirements. So the inspiration comes from those requirements. In my work with electric instruments I am particularly drawn to the requirements of ergonomics. I have found that physical prototyping is the method that works best for me. And so my designs are the results of an iterative process of hypothesizing desired effect, building prototypes, and testing them with real musicians. To me, the resulting instruments have a strong form-follows-function aspect to their appearance, which (I hope!) is thought to be aesthetically pleasing as well.

That said, I would be remiss if I didn't point out that sometimes my designs are completely driven by whimsy, and some of those seem to work well, too. There is certainly room for all approaches to instrument design, and there is certainly no single right way to go about doing it.

R.M. Mottola is one of the most recognized names in the research-oriented musical instrument design circles. He also conducts research in the areas of acoustics, psychoacoustics, ergonomics, materials and construction. The bass in the picture is his *Mezzaluna* model ("Mezzaluna" is Italian word for "half moon"): The name comes from the wide waist cutout, which allows the instrument to be played resting on the leg in a superior ergonomic position.

2) Playability, sound, beauty: list them ordered by importance.

All these factors are important of course, so for me the question really comes down to the sequence in which I apply these during the design process. In general, as described above, I go for playability first and foremost. I've found that tone never has to be compromised for the sake of playability. As a palette for creativity, the solid body electric guitar family is particularly appealing for this reason. It is rarely difficult to design electric instruments such that they can be fitted with a wide variety of mechanical hardware, pickups and controls. And pickup and electronics manufacturers offer a wide variety of products and are generally very willing to work with builders to meet our particular requirements.

I do hope that what I have written above does not imply that I consider aesthetic beauty to be of least importance. But I generally do take a more form-follows-function approach to my designs and trust that the inherent beauty of such designs shines through.

3) What makes your designs unique?

When I look at all of the wonderful instruments available today, I can't help but observe that all are unique and all reflect upon their designers. This variety to me is the true richness of modern lutherie. My instruments are unique for the same reason that all other luthiers' instruments are unique. Each was designed by a person with a unique background, personality, and their own unique approach to lutherie. In my observation, this individuality shines through even in very constrained types of instruments, such as, say, Strat copies. And sometimes, working in a highly constrained area like that, the individuality is even more apparent, because the designer has to concentrate his or her expression in seemingly very small things.

Ralph Novak

1) What inspires you? How do the ideas come to you?

Inspiration is drawn from many sources when I build "for myself" (more on this later...). When an instrument is built to order, however, it is a collaboration of the designer and the player's purpose and goals. The inspiration comes from working within the player's requirements while attempting to somehow go beyond the design goal and create something truly exciting–something that moves the player and listener on a deep level. I must humbly admit that I'm not always successful in this–it's a somewhat indescribable quality, and there's no set process to achieve it. If I have achieved it with some of my instruments, then I'm quite pleased, as are the players.

Regarding the instruments I referred to as "for myself," let me say that, while I have a business built on serving the player, I admit I sometimes just have to build something that's my own concept–"just for fun," so to speak. I enjoy building guitars and like to "play" with design concepts, unique woods, and ideas that come from many places, including music itself. After

A Robert Armstrong caricature of **Ralph Novak**. His instruments have several unusual design features, which beyond an appealing aesthetic, are primarily described as performance-enhancers: in particular, the *"Fanned-Frets"* guitars.

all, if I can't build for "fun," why would I do it?

Additionally, there's the inspiration that comes from attempting to achieve an "ideal," an artistic vision that perhaps is not even fully crystallized but begs to be brought to life. That vision might be "musical," such as "can I achieve a certain sound that I hear as beautiful or enchanting"; or it may be "visual," such as a combination of "lines" and woods that evoke a feeling in the viewer. That's a special moment of inspiration when I'm moved to make something that challenges me to reach a bit farther.

2) Playability, sound, and beauty: list them ordered by importance.

I believe you've listed them in the appropriate order, as I see it. I am, after all, building instruments that must ultimately be played, so, if I absolutely must choose an order to list these characteristics, then playability must come first. This in no way diminishes the importance of either tone or beauty, it just emphasizes that these "objects" we make are musical instruments and not just "art." They must be able to be used effectively if tone and beauty are to be considered.

3) What makes your designs unique?

I believe the most obvious characteristic of my designs is the Fanned-Fret concept and its blending, artistically and functionally, into traditional electric guitar and bass aesthetic. My quest for "tone" is evident in my choices of scale lengths and my proprietary individual bridge system. Certainly my tonal ideas are not in concert with many of my contemporaries; I believe this has informed my aesthetic as well as my engineering and design. I'm not attempting to recreate a glorious past—I'm about forging a bold future where the player has more creative freedom and individuality.

Claudio and Claudia Pagelli

1) What inspires you? When/how do the ideas come to you?

Everything is inspiring... flowers, the view from our apartment in the mountains, fabric patterns, a cooking pot, paintings, photos, children laughs, stones, wood, good wine and conversation, walking, music, flea markets, relaxation... Be open-minded—"impossible" (mostly) doesn't exist.

Ideas come to us always and everywhere: surprising, gathered, discussed, drawn, skizzed, spontaneous... as a feeling that develops itself, mainly as visualization. But when we build a special instrument for someone, his/her ideas and design are respected and considered by talking with the customer: preferences, interests, destinations, culture, "gold or silver?", favorite movies, etc

2) Playability, tone, and beauty: If you must list these three characteristics by importance, how would you order them?

First, sound and playability: The instrument has priority. The appearance is the intention to bring together the resultant shapes and desires and transforming them attractively for the customer. The Holy Trinity:

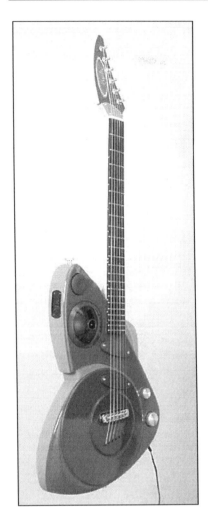

Sound, Playability, Looks—the design has to be the connection.

Of course we have instruments originating through purely visual ideas, mostly our prototypes. But the looks must not prevail over the instrument. We build instruments, not "cult" or artistic objects. If they mutate into that, it does not depend on us...

3) What makes your designs unique?

We emphasize finding new ways, but keeping the instrument true to itself. What most differentiate us is that we don't have just one design, or instrument type, that makes us known. Pagelli is known because we build the whole palette: electric guitars and basses, acoustic and jazz guitars. And, so far, they are all unique pieces. We don't use serial numbers. We aim at delivering the highest quality, and not only for the customer, but also because we want to improve ourselves, up to the last detail... and it has been like that for 30 years, already!

Sebastian Heck

1) What inspires you? How do the ideas come to you?

My main inspiration is the simple fact that there are very few good designs on the market. Most manufacturers copy the successful instruments of Fender and Gibson without having the courage to develop their own designs. In most cases, I get the ideas from quite ordinary things, everyday life items. I look at them and suddenly I see an interesting shape, and then I try to make a good design out of it... Other times I'm just sitting at my desk with a pen and a blank sheet of paper and start sketching.

2) Playability, sound, and beauty: list them ordered by importance.

That depends on the musician. I think sound and playability (in this order) are the most important things on a guitar. But I try to package both characteristics into a good-looking design. That's the main challenge.

3) What makes your designs unique?

A quite difficult question! When I develop a design, the primary requirement is the customer's expectation. Therefore the design shows also the style and the likings of the customer; the result is a mixture of the customers' ideas and my own style.

When I design without any customer-specifications, my designs mostly turn out to look modern—I don't know how to describe it, perhaps you could call it "clean", "straight" even. And I like that kind of reverse-look (I call it "inverse Pagelli style"), but without any Mosrite-affiliations.

For me it's also very important to stay flexible and not be caught in my own too-special style.

Sebastian Heck was born in 1977 in Stuttgart, and his first contact with popular music was a TV-show about The Beatles. He started playing guitar in the mid 90s, until he took part in a workshop about guitar design and couldn't stop anymore. In 2008 he started www.gitarrendesign.de

Ralf Martens

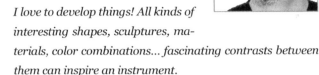

1) What inspires you? When/how do the ideas come to you?

I love to develop things! All kinds of interesting shapes, sculptures, materials, color combinations... fascinating contrasts between them can inspire an instrument.

Many ideas come spontaneously, playing with the forms, or through objects that can be seen or touch, and many others ideas are strenuously developed.

Sometimes is about a simple dissatisfaction with conventional solutions.

2) Playability, sound, and beauty: list them ordered by importance.

Playability, tone, looks. Ideally, all of them harmonizing with each other.

3) What makes your designs unique? What do you think is your differential against the rest of the world?

They are mirrors of my fundamental personality, and consequently, unique. They are my subjective perception of a guitar or a bass.

Born in '65, Ralf became interested in drawing and product design many years ago. Playing guitar and learning how to build aircrafts were symptoms of an underlying desire: to design guitars. He met Sebastian Heck on an online guitarmaking forum, with whom he joined forces behind the helm of `gitarrendesign.de`, one of the most resourceful guitar design websites .

Martin Off

1) What inspires you? How do the ideas come to you?

It may sound funny, but the inspiration comes from almost everywhere: sometimes there is a motto or an idea–for instance, the idea to make a "Glamour Guitar", so then the "show" aspect is the guiding concept. Besides my job as a designer, I like to paint as well, so art itself inspires me. Visiting art exhibitions brings me ideas. Sometimes it is the mixture of vintage items like those cheap and cheesy pawnshop guitars, or ancient cars on one hand and modern design items on the other hand. And finally–looking at beautiful pieces of wood–that instantly inspires me to turn that thing into a beautiful guitar.

2) Playability, sound, and beauty: list them ordered by importance.

First, tone. We're talking about making music, so of course tone is number one. A guitar can look gorgeous,

An independent designer and illustrator from Germany, Martin Off designed his first guitar in 2002. Since then, he won several design contests with his instruments, being the most important the ones organized by the prestigious Gitarre & Bass Magazine. In the picture, the beautiful, award winning "Miss Blues" model.

but if it doesn't sound good, you better hang it on the wall and enjoy the looks.

A close second, beauty. For me is important to find new, sometimes "weird" contours and create something you would look good with on stage.

Third, playability. I would dare to say the shape of a neck, the neck heel, an excellent fret setup, a perfect action, and trusty tuners makes 90% of playability. If these components fit your taste, playing is comfortable almost automatically.

The rest is for looks, especially the body shapes—sometimes the guitar body may fit your body like a glove (that's perfect ergonomics)—and sometimes it might hurt a bit. You wouldn't say that an Explorer or a Flying V are the most ergonomic designs, would you? You choose it because of a certain attitude and because they look cool!

3) What makes your designs unique? What do you think is your differential against the rest of the world?

I simply try to create new and maybe a bit weird designs. I would say they are modern with a bit of vintage/retro touch to it. I'm not interested in copying some of the classics, neither in making something like an "almost-like-a Strat" thing.

I guess it's really about finding new forms and to create something a bit more bold, thrilling, and sexy. Yes, my goal is designing very sexy guitars!

Appendix B

WOOD SPECIES USED IN LUTHERIE

Some of the species traditionally used for electric guitar making are described in the following pages, together with a summary of their physical characteristics, geographical distribution, alternative names, most common name in other languages, reported toxicity and hazardousness, and current environmental situation [41]. For each species, a short review of the way they respond to common woodworking tasks is included.

Alder		Density	Toxicity / Hazard	Environmental concern	
		0,41	Dermatitis	Not reported	
(Alnus Rubra)	German: Erle			Laminated tops:	Y
	Italian: Aliso	Hardness		Bodies:	Y
Europe, Russia, Western Asia, Japan. Red Alder: US, Canada.	Spanish Alno	590		Necks:	N
	French: Aulne			Fretboards:	N

Straight grained, fine textured, orange brown sapwood and heartwood with no outstanding figure. Moderately heavy and soft with low bending strength, shock resistance, stiffness, and decay resistance. Nails, screws, glues, and works well. Stains and polishes satisfactorily.

Ash	Biltmore Ash, cane Ash, Biltmore Ash	Density	Toxicity / Hazard	Environmental concern	
		0,54	Decrease in lung function	Not reported	
(Fraxinus Americana)	German: Esche			Laminated tops:	Y
	Italian: Frassino	Hardness		Bodies:	Y
United States and Canada	Spanish Fresno	1320		Necks:	N
	French: Frêne			Fretboards:	N

Generally straight grained with a coarse texture. Pale-brown heartwood and almost white sapwood. Moderately heavy, hard, strong, and tough with moderately high shock resistance, good dimensional stability, and poor decay resistance. Steam-bends very well and is quite elastic. Machines fairly well. Glues, screws, and nails satisfactorily. Stains and finishes well, although filling may be required.

---

[41] *Source: CITES–Convention on International Trade in Endangered Species of Wild Fauna and Flora*

Basswood

	Lime, Beetree, Linn, Linden	Density	Toxicity / Hazard	Environmental concern	
(Tilia Americana)	German: *Linde*	**0,8**	Irritant of the eyes, skin, and respiratory system.	Not reported	
	Italian: *Tiglio*	Hardness		Laminated tops:	N
United States and Canada	Spanish: *Tilo*			Bodies:	N
	French: *Tilleul*	**410**		Necks:	Y
				Fretboards:	N

Generally straight grained with a fine, uniform texture and medium luster. Creamy-white to brownish heartwood and nearly white sapwood. Soft, light, low in strength, shock resistance and decay resistance. Poor for steam bending. Works well with sharp machine or hand tools and is excellent for carving (soft and resists splitting). Glues, screws, nails, stains, and finishes satisfactorily although its soft texture can be challenging for staining.

Bubinga

	Akume, Kevazingo, Ovang, Waka, Etimoé	Density	Toxicity / Hazard	Environmental concern	
(Gibourtia tessmannii)	German: *Bubinga*	**0,8**	Dermatitis, possible skin lessions	VULNERABLE	
	Italian: *Bubinga*	Hardness		Laminated tops:	Y
West Africa	Spanish: *Bubinga*			Bodies:	Y
	French: *Bubinga*	**2690**		Necks:	Y
				Fretboards:	Y

The grain may be straight or interlocked. Even texture ranging from fine to very fine. Whitish sapwood, medium red-brown or red to reddish-brown heartwood, with lighter red to purple veins. Upon exposure, the wood becomes yellow or medium brown with a reddish tint, and the veining becomes less conspicuous. The wood is lustrous. Unpleasant odor when is freshly cut. The wood exerts moderate to severe blunting effect on cutters. Bubinga is hard and heavy, saws slowly but readily. A reduced planing angle of 15 degrees is recommended to prevent irregular and interlocked grain from tearing or picking up. Boring and routing properties and carving properties are generally good. Gluing qualities are rather poor because of gum pockets. Pre-boring required before screwing. It sands well and takes an excellent polish.

Cocobolo

	Granadillo, Caviuna, Jacaranda, Nambar	Density	Toxicity / Hazard	Environmental concern	
(Dalbergia Retusa)	German: *Cocobolo*	**1,11**	Dermatitis, nose and throat irritant, conjunctivitis, bronchial asthma, nausea (potent)	Not reported	
	Italian: *Cocobolo*	Hardness		Laminated tops:	Y
Central America	Spanish: *Cocobolo*			Bodies:	N
	French: *Cocobolo*	**1136**		Necks:	N
				Fretboards:	Y

The grain is usually straight and fine textured. The color of the heartwood varies when freshly-cut, and is described as a rainbow-hued. It saws readily with only a slight blunting effect on cutting edges. Moderate blunting effect on tools. Cutting edges must be kept sharp. Mostly unsuitable for gluing because it contains natural oils. Oil in the wood gives it a fine natural polish. A smooth and waxy surface can be achieved by rubbing the wood with a cloth without using any finishes.

Ebony

	Mgiriti, Msindi, Kanran, Nyareti, Kukuo,	Density	Toxicity / Hazard	Environmental concern	
(Diospyros Kamerunensis)	German: *Ebenholz*	**1,04**	Skin irritation, dermatitis	VULNERABLE	
	Italian: *Ebano*	Hardness		Laminated tops:	N
Southern Africa	Spanish: *Ébano*			Bodies:	N
	French: *Ébène*	**3220**		Necks:	N
				Fretboards:	Y

Hard and heavy, causes severe dulling effect on cutting edges. Chips easily. It is difficult to work in planing and most operations. It is an excellent turnery wood, and carves very well. Is reported to be difficult to glue. Polishing properties are excellent.

Koa

			Density	Toxicity / Hazard	Environmental concern	
	Hawaiian mahogany, Hawaiian Acacia		**0,67**	No information available. Toxic effects reported in animals (alopecia, rushes)	Not reported	
(Acacia Koa)	German:	Koa			Laminated tops:	Y
	Italian:	Koa	Hardness		Bodies:	Y
Hawaii	Spanish	Acacia Koa			Necks:	Y
	French:	Koa	**1220**		Fretboards:	N

Wavy, curly grain, moderate to severely interlocked. Light and dark bands in the growth rings. The grain produces various attractive patterns. The texture is moderately coarse. The sapwood is pale brown, clearly demarcated from the heartwood, commonly reddish brown. Highly lustrous surface. Difficult to saw because of interlocked grain. Tools should be kept sharp to prevent tearouts. The wood has medium blunting effect on tools. Responds well to hand and machine tools. End-grain material requires very sharp cutting edges. Gluing properties generally poor. Takes stain and varnish very well.

Korina

			Density	Toxicity / Hazard	Environmental concern	
	Limba, Fakre, Fraké, Afara, White Afara		**0,55**	Splinters go septic, nose and gum bleeding, decrease in lung function	Not reported	
(Terminalia Superba)	German:	Korina			Laminated tops:	Y
	Italian:	Korina	Hardness		Bodies:	Y
Tropical Western Africa	Spanish	Korina			Necks:	N
	French:	Korina	**490**		Fretboards:	N

Straight to irregular or interlocked grain. Texture is moderately coarse. Colors: uniformly cream, pale yellow or grayish brown; irregular streaks which give the wood an attractive appearance. Wood surface has a high, satiny luster. Slight dulling effect on cutting edges. Responds well to ordinary machining tools in all operations. Gluing properties are satisfactory. Pre-boring is required since the wood has a tendency to split. Take stains readily. Polishing qualities are excellent after filling.

Lacewood

			Density	Toxicity / Hazard	Environmental concern	
	Silky Oak, Selena, Selano, Louro Faia		**0,6**	Sawdust causes skin irritation, respiratory problems, dermatitis	Not reported	
(Cardwellia sublimis)	German:	Grevillea			Laminated tops:	Y
	Italian:		Hardness		Bodies:	Y
Australia	Spanish	Roble aust.			Necks:	Y
	French:	Grevillea	**840**		Fretboards:	N

Variable grain with large rays, specially visible in quartersawn pieces, which gives its "reptilian" appearance. Reddish brown color with a moderately coarse even texture. Wood matures to a brownish color with age. Good workability. The rays may tend to tear out. Accepts finishes well.

Mahogany

			Density	Toxicity / Hazard	Environmental concern	
	True Mahogany, Honduras mahagony		**0,65**	Skin irritation, giddiness, vomiting, furunculosis, pheumonitis, alveolitis	ENDANGERED	
Honduras	German:	Mahagoni			Laminated tops:	Y
(Swietenia Macrophylla)	Italian:	Mogano	Hardness		Bodies:	Y
Central and South America	Spanish	Caoba			Necks:	Y
	French:	Acajou	**800**		Fretboards:	N

The grain varies from straight to roey, wavy, or curly. Irregularities in the grain often produce highly attractive figures. The texture is fine or medium to coarse, and uniform. Dark colored gum or white deposits may be present in the pores. Mahogany varies considerably in color, which has enabled many look-alike species to be marketed as mahogany. Low stiffness and shock resistance. Excellent working properties. Finishes easily, although filling may be required.

Mahogany

	Khaya		Density	Toxicity / Hazard	Environmental concern	
African	German:	*Mahagoni*	**0,5**	Skin irritation, giddiness, vomits, furunculosis, pheumonitis, alveolitis	Not reported	
(Khaya Ivorensis)	Italian:	*Mogano*			Laminated tops:	Y
West Africa	Spanish	*Caoba*	Hardness		Bodies:	Y
					Necks:	Y
	French:	*Acajou*	**830**		Fretboards:	N

Straight grain with a fine even texture. Reddish brown to medium red. Interlocked or straight grain, often with a ribbon figure, and a moderately coarse texture. Moderately heavy and hard with medium bending and crushing strength, low stiffness and shock resistance. Glues, nails, and screws satisfactorily. Stains and polishes to an excellent finish.

Mahogany

	Sapele, Sapelli		Density	Toxicity / Hazard	Environmental concern	
African	German:	*Mahagoni*	**0,5**	Skin irritation, giddiness, vomits, furunculosis, pheumonitis, alveolitis	Not reported	
(Entandrophragma cylindricum)	Italian:	*Mogano*			Laminated tops:	Y
West, Central and East Africa	Spanish	*Caoba*	Hardness		Bodies:	Y
					Necks:	Y
	French:	*Acajou*	**1510**		Fretboards:	N

Interlocked, sometimes wavy grain producing a distinctive roe figure on quartered surfaces. Medium texture, high luster. Medium weight, crushing strength and shock resistance. Low stiffness. Works easily enough although surface may tear when planing due to interlocked grain. Glues, screws, and nails satisfactorily. Responds well to stains and finishes, particularly if grain is filled.

Maple

			Density	Toxicity / Hazard	Environmental concern	
(Acer spp.)	German:	*Ahorn*	**0,65**	Decrease in lung function	Not reported	
	Italian:	*Acero*			Laminated tops:	Y
	Spanish	*Arce*	Hardness		Bodies:	Y
Asia, Europe, northern Africa, and North America.					Necks:	Y
	French:	*Érable*	**1450**		Fretboards:	Y

Tipically straight grain, close and subdued. Extremely attractive figure sometimes, including, bird's eye, maple burl, blistered, leaf, and fiddleback. Straight, close grain with a fine, uniform texture. Pre-drilling recommended for screwing or nailing. Glues well and finishes very smoothly. There are four classifications of maple commonly used in lutherie. **Eastern hard maple** (sugar maple) is used for Fender guitar necks. It is hard, heavy and abrasion resistant. **Eastern soft maple** (constituting about 5 species) is sometimes used for solid bodies. It is not too hard, not too heavy, not too abrasion resistant. **European maple** (constituting one or two species) is similar to eastern soft maple and is not used in the USA for solid body guitars; **Western bigleaf maple** is moderately heavy, moderately hard and stringy in texture. It is often figured and is used for drop tops.

Padauk

	Padouk, Barwood, Mbe Mbil, Camwood, Corail		Density	Toxicity / Hazard	Environmental concern	
(Pterocarpus soyauxii)	German:		**0,38**	Skin irrittation, pheumonitis, alveolitis (potent and common).	*Pt. indicus* is at risk	
	Italian:	*Paduk*			Laminated tops:	Y
Central and West Africa	Spanish		Hardness		Bodies:	N
					Necks:	N
	French:	*Padouk*	**1725**		Fretboards:	Y

Open, straight dark grain. Moderately coarse texture and large pores. Rich red to purple heartwood and pale-beige sapwood. The wood routs and recess fairly easily. Glues very well. Screw-holding qualities are rated as good, but stock in smaller dimensions may split in screwing. Good sanding qualities. Water-based finishes have been reported to hold color better.

Poplar

		Density	Toxicity / Hazard	Environmental concern	
Poplar	Yellow Poplar, Tulip Poplar, Tulipwood	**0,46**	Sneezing, eye irritation, may cause blisters	Not reported	
(Liriodendron tulipifera)	German: *Pappel*			Laminated tops:	Y
	Italian: *Pioppo*	Hardness		Bodies:	Y
North America, Europe, Asia	Spanish: *Tulipero, Tulipanero*	**540**		Necks:	N
	French: *Peuplier*			Fretboards:	N

Generally straight grained and "woolly" with a fine, even texture. Most species are typically soft and light with low ratings for strength, stiffness and shock resistance. Works easily with hand or machine tools but sharp edges recommended. Glues, screws and nails well. Staining can be patchy but paints and varnish are easily applied.

Redwood

		Density	Toxicity / Hazard	Environmental concern	
Redwood	California Redwood, Sequioa, Vavona	**0,42**	Skin irrittation, pheumonitis, alveolitis	Not reported	
(Sequoia sempervirens)	German: *Redwood, Maser*			Laminated tops:	Y
	Italian: *Sequioa*	Hardness		Bodies:	N
California and Oregon	Spanish: *Secoya, Secuoya*	**420**		Necks:	N
	French: *Sequioa*			Fretboards:	N

Generally straight grain with a fine to coarse texture. Very prominent growth rings. Generally straight grained with a fine to coarse texture. Very prominent growth rings. Light and soft with moderately low bending and crushing strength, low shock resistance, moderate stiffness. Works easily with hand or machine tools but has some tendency to splinter. Screws easily but has poor holding properties. Glues quite satisfactorily. Accepts and holds paints exceptionally well.

Rosewood

		Density	Toxicity / Hazard	Environmental concern	
Rosewood	Bombay, Shisham, Malabar, Sissoo, Biti	**0,88**	Dermatitis, respiratory disorders (very potent)	Not reported	
Indian	German:			Laminated tops:	Y
(Dalbergia latifolia)	Italian: *Palissandro India*	Hardness		Bodies:	Y
Southern India	Spanish: *Palisandro*	**3170**		Necks:	Y
	French: *palissandre*			Fretboards:	Y

Commonly interlocked grain with a uniform, moderately coarse texture. Commonly interlocked grain with a uniform, moderately coarse texture. Heavy, hard, and dense with high bending and crushing strengths, medium shock resistance, good stability and very durable heartwood. Difficult to work due to calcareous deposits - dulls cutting edges. Holds screws well and glues satisfactorily. Finishes nicely although filling recommended.

Rosewood

		Density	Toxicity / Hazard	Environmental concern	
Rosewood		**0,51**	Dermatitis, respiratory disorders (very potent)	Not reported	
Indonesian	German: *Palisander*			Laminated tops:	Y
(Dalbergia Stevensonii)	Italian: *Palisandro*	Hardness		Bodies:	Y
India, and as introduced species, in Nigeria.	Spanish: *Palisandro*	**1720**		Necks:	Y
	French: *palissandre*			Fretboards:	Y

The crossed or narrowly interlocked grain. Combination of darker streaks of color and interlocked grain give the timber a very attractive appearance. The texture is moderately coarse and uniform. Luster varies from dull to medium. The freshly cut wood is characterized by a fragrant scent. There is no distinctive odor after the material is seasoned. Very difficult to work with, tends to dull cutters. Very poor bending properties.

Rosewood

Brazilian

(Dalbergia Nigra)

Brazil

Rio Rosewood, Caviuna, Obuina		Density	Toxicity / Hazard	Environmental concern	
German:	Palisander	**0,55**	Contains Juglone, a chemical which might cause dermatitis	ENDANGERED	
Italian:	Palisandro Rio			Laminated tops:	Y
Spanish	Palisandro Brasil	Hardness		Bodies:	Y
French:	Palissandre Rio	**2720**		Necks:	Y
				Fretboards:	N

Most straight grain with coarse texture, large open pores, and oil, gritty feel. Mostly straight grained with coarse texture, large open pores, and oil, gritty feel. Cream-colored sapwood. Hard and heavy, moderate to high strength and shock resistance, low stiffness. Causes severe blunting effect on cutting edges. Pre-drilling recommended for screws. Glues satisfactorily if precautions taken for oily surfaces (consider using epoxy resins). Finishes to an exceedingly smooth, highly polished surface.

Walnut

(Juglans nigra)

United States and Canada

Nussbaum		Density	Toxicity / Hazard	Environmental concern	
German:	Walnuss	**0,83**	Eyes and skin irritation. Frequency: common.	Not reported	
Italian:	Noce Nero			Laminated tops:	Y
Spanish	Nogal	Hardness		Bodies:	Y
French:	Noyer Noir	**1010**		Necks:	Y
				Fretboards:	Y

Generally straight grained with a moderately coarse, uniform texture. Rich dark brown heartwood and nearly white sapwood. Generally straight grained with a moderately coarse, uniform texture. Moderately heavy, hard, strong, and stiff. Works very well with machine or hand tools. Excels at routing, shaping, carving, and drilling. Sands easily and finishes to a velvety, natural-colored sheen.

Wenge

(Milettia laurentii)

Africa (Zaire, Cameroon, Gabon, Tanzania, Mozambique, Congo)

Awoung, Dikela, Mibotu, Bokonge		Density	Toxicity / Hazard	Environmental concern	
German:	Wengé, Wenge	**0,88**	Splinters go septic, dermatitis, nervous system effects abdominal cramps	ENDANGERED	
Italian:	Wengé			Laminated tops:	Y
Spanish	Wenge	Hardness		Bodies:	N
French:	Wengé	**1630**		Necks:	N
				Fretboards:	N

Very dark, with a very distinctive figure, and a strong "partridge" pattern. The wood exerts medium blunting effect on cutting tools. Saws slowly, but works fairly easy with machine tools. Rather difficult to glue because of the presence of resin cells. Tough and strong timber, requires pre-boring in nailing, but holding characteristics are good. Sands satisfactorily. Difficult to polish, varnishes poorly. Some solvent-based stained resins dry with difficulty. The wood responds well to hand tools.

Zebrano

(Microberlinia brazzavillensis)

Western Africa, mainly Cameroon and Gabon

Zebrawood, Amouk Zingana, Allen ele		Density	Toxicity / Hazard	Environmental concern	
German:	Zingana	**0,74**	Eyes and skin irritation	ENDANGERED	
Italian:	Zingano			Laminated tops:	Y
Spanish		Hardness		Bodies:	N
French:	Zingana	**1575**		Necks:	N
				Fretboards:	N

Moderately coarse texture, close defined grain. Yellow brown heartwood, light sapwood with a dark contrasting grain which gives this wood its zebra like appearence. Fair - Veneers are fragile. Grain can tend to tear when planing. Good gluing properties. Fair grain tend to be prone to wear. Veneer tends to be fragile and can break easily.

Appendix C

PICKUP COLOR CODES

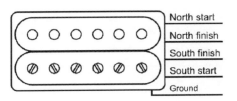

Anderson	Bartolini	Benedetto	Di Marzio
Red	Black	Red	Red
Green	Red	Black	Black
White	White	White	White
Black	Green	Green	Green

EMG-HZ	Fender	Gibson	Gotoh
Red	Green	Red	Black
Black	White	White	White
White	Black	Green	Red
Green	Red	Black	Green

Ibanez	Jackson	Schaller	S. Duncan
Red	Green	Yellow	Black
Black	White	Brown	White
White	Red	White	Red
Blue	Black	Green	Green

B. Knuckle	B. Lawrence	Peavey	Shadow
Red	Red	Red	Green
Green	White	Green	White
White	Green	White	Brown
Black	Black	Black	Yellow

PRS	WD/Kent Armstrong	Lindy Fralin	Barden
Red	Green	White	Black
Black	White	Green	White
White	Black/Blue	Red	Red
Red	Red/Pink	Black	Green

Appendix D
PICKUP CAVITIES TEMPLATES

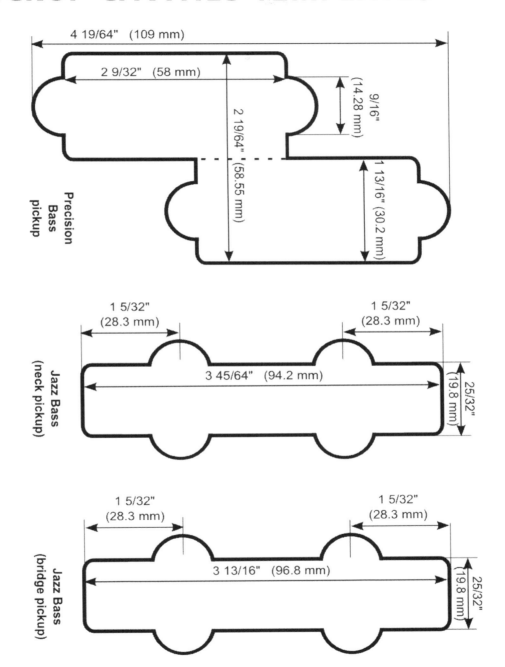

You can base your blueprint on these templates and measurements. When building your instrument, however, get some real pickup cavity templates in order to avoid any errors and to rout a precise, "clean" cavity.

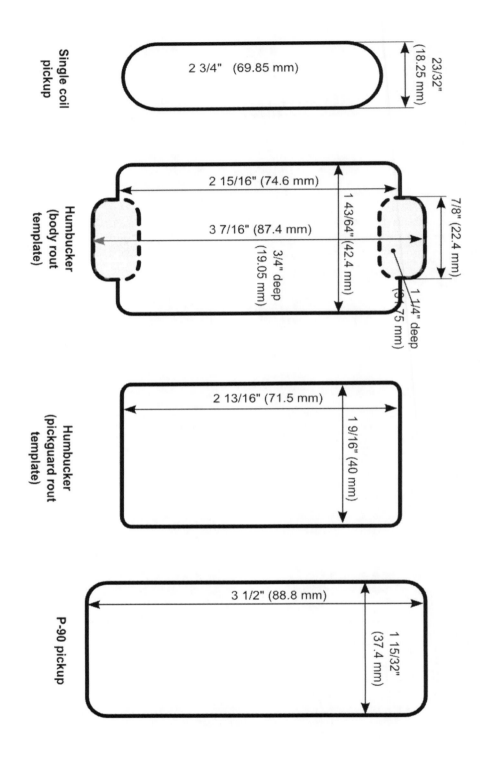

Single coil pickup

2 3/4" (69.85 mm)

23/32" (18.25 mm)

Humbucker (body rout template)

2 15/16" (74.6 mm)

1 43/64" (42.4 mm)

3 7/16" (87.4 mm)

3/4" deep (19.05 mm)

7/8" (22.4 mm)

1 1/4" deep (9.75 mm)

Humbucker (pickguard rout template)

2 13/16" (71.5 mm)

1 9/16" (40 mm)

P-90 pickup

3 1/2" (88.8 mm)

1 15/32" (37.4 mm)

TABLE OF CONTENTS

Function of the headstock - Headstock shapes - Headstock dimensions - Headstock angle - Headstock joint - Tuning machines–Tuners placement - Strings "headstock path" - No headstock at all! - How to design a great headstock - Neck / headstock joint

Ergonomics: A definition - Guitar ergonomics - The guitar body: 3D considerations - The guitar's body edges - Ergonomics while playing standing - Ergonomics while playing seated - Improving ergonomics - 3D prototypes

Neck back shapes - The old fellas and the new kids on the block - Neck depth - Standard measurements–Neck depth - Neck angle and its relation to the guitar top - Pros and cons of using an angled neck - The truss rod - Truss rod types - Truss rod adjustment access point - Which length? - How many truss rods?

How many strings? - Fretboard main dimensions–Scale - Standard guitar scales - Standard bass scales - String spread at the nut - String setback - Width at the nut - Fretted or fretless? - How many frets? - Standard measurements–Number of frets - Placement of the frets - Fretwire anatomy - Choosing fretwire - Fretwire material - Fretwire height - Fretwire Width - Fretboard radius - Conical (compound) radius fretboards - Special fretboards - Scalloped fretboards - Multi-scale fretboards - How to build a neck for great playability

How do pickups work? - Magnets and their influence on the sound, Coils and their influence on the sound - Standard coil turn numbers - Interaction between magnet and coil - Humbucking pickups - *The Secrets of Electric Guitar Pickup (by Helmuth Lemme)* - The pickup as a circuit - How Resonance Affects Sound - Single coil vs. humbuckers response - Summary

Matching pickups - Solo switching - Matching passive and active pickups - Pickup placement - *What is the* practical *way to place pickups?* - Slanted pickups - Pickup cavities

Philosophy of control design - Volume control - The problem with independent controls for each pickup - Blender control–The problem with blender controls - Tone control (or equalization controls) - No controls at all!–Switches–Pickup selection - Coil Tapping–Mod setting - Switches used on electric guitars - Toggle switches - Lever switches - Rotary switches–Knobs - Jack plate - Control placement - Well designed controls -

Electronic components–Potentiometers - Pot value - Pot taper - Push/pull" and "push/push" pots - Dual concentric controls - How potentiometers affect sound - Use of capacitors for tone control - How capacitors affect the resonant frequency - Drawing the wiring diagram - The block diagram -

Connecting components - How to connect a volume pot - How to wire tone pots - How to wire dual concentric pots - How to wire switches for pickup selection - How to wire a jack - Ground connection–Shielding - Grounding of the bridge - Advice for avoiding electrical shock - Wiring diagrams: examples - Precision Bass wiring - One of the simplest options for a guitar - Stratocaster wiring - Gibson's wiring (Les Paul, SG, 335, etc.) - Gibsons with 3 pickups - Jazz Bass wiring - PRS wiring with rotary switch - Active electronics - Active circuit pros and cons - Control cavity - Rear controls cavity cover - Control cavity depth - Choosing the electronic components

Printed in Great Britain
by Amazon